I0137528

HOLLYWOOD MYSTERIES

TRUE STORIES OF SCANDAL AND MYSTERY

by

CHARLES NUETZEL

The Borgo Press
An Imprint of Wildside Press

MMVII

BORGO BIOVIEWS
ISSN 0743-0628

Number Seven

Copyright © 1965, 1969, 2007 by Charles Nuetzel

All rights reserved.
No part of this book may be reproduced in any form
without the expressed written consent
of the author and publisher.
Printed in the United States of America

FIRST EDITION

CONTENTS

INTRODUCTION

It has been said that Hollywood is a city of vice and sin, of immorality, of wild parties where every young starlet lays down her body as the Price for a movie role. These same people claim it's a cesspool for Gays, for the quick marriage-divorce which is nothing more than legalized sex; where the kings and queens of the syndicated newspaper columns dictate to the studio bosses because of their power to make or break a star. That's the way it used to be.

Hollywood was the center of the world's movie industry long enough to have made its name immortal. It is a legend which created legends, both past and present. Even today Hollywood, with all its faults and virtues, is the dream factory where flesh peddlers sit in their plush offices and dole out a continuing stream of celluloid fantasy to be gobbled up by a world starving for escapism.

People have come from all over the globe to seek their fame and fortune in the movie industry, paying the price in emotions, hunger and pain. And what about these people who hunger to become a part of the Hollywood legend? Some have talent, some have only beautiful bodies to offer. All have a craving desire to make it to the top. Even today, in the twenty-first century, young actors, by the thousands, flock to Hollywood and pound the doors of agents, producers, casting directors and writers.

Hollywood has been criticized for its lack of morality, for its abuse of innocent struggling actors. Power brokers still make use of the "casting couch" to satisfy their base hungers. Too many struggling actors are willing to do anything to get their first break. "Just give me a chance," is what they beg of anybody willing to listen.

And it hasn't changed much since I wrote this book about the early years of Hollywood. What was fascinating to me was the discovery of how films helped to shape our culture and lives–and how Hollywood itself changed its public moral flavor over the decades. From sin city to prude town (on film only)! It still remained the basic human landscape that took advantage of the young and innocent in their hungry grab at success and fame.

It has been said that it is possible to make a star of anyone. It only takes a lot of money and a lot of promotion. Even then, there are very few who become a Gable, Brando, Burton, Taylor, Flynn, Monroe, or Landis. Those super stars of yesterday, at the very beginning years when Hollywood was truly the film center of the world!

Talent has very little to do with this kind of success. It is part of it, sure, but not the totality. Talent can be cheap! It takes a lot more; like timing, luck, connections, and a wild determination to win at any price! And the cost can be heavy.

Unless you are born in the business, or have friends in the business, or you have enough money to promote yourself, the cold facts are that no matter how much talent you may have, no one is really interested. Not in you. Their attention is on the fast buck, the successful investment. After that comes the art, the creative force and drives and aims of those given control over very expensive productions. It takes a very special type of person to struggle through the obstacle course to stardom. It takes a person with drive which will keep going in spite of all odds, regardless of price.

A young talent has to be seen by the right people. He must know the right people. The quest for success takes time, loneliness, struggling, anguish, guts and that driving force which sets aside all other considerations. One might call this drive a form of blind, emotional insanity. If the Hollywood promoters notice you, they will take over your life, direct your every action, both on and off the screen. The public will be fed an endless diet of publicity material. It takes a special type of emotional balance to be willing to go through all the frustrations which lead to fame and fortune.

And even as a big named super star you are required to make the promotional circuits, the television shows, to be endlessly interviewed. Many times you have a nice slice of the action to sweeten the pot. For a big name gets the money people willing to back a film production.

Money, money, money. It hasn't changed. It is all about money.

And even the most talented, creative, artistically centered people find it necessary to cater to the accountants and the bankers and the investors' interest only in their percentage, their profit.

The young hopeful is faced with several cold facts when he first arrives in Hollywood.

The town itself is outwardly no different than any other town: streets, buildings, homes, banks, shopping centers. There is no glittering gold, no glamour, no warmth. The important people are protected. Their offices are harder to get into than the White House. The unions are tight with no apparent way to get in. Agents aren't interested in anyone who isn't a *working* actor or actress.

No matter what parents and friends think of you back home, Hollywood doesn't care if you live or die. You are friendless, jobless, and aren't about to be "discovered."

The Hollywood legend tries to make believe that all you have to do is walk into a drug store, have a soda and bang, all of a sudden your are a Lana Turner. It's really not quite that easy.

A young actor or actress will live a lonely life filled with frustrations and seemingly endless periods of waiting. The interminable silence which fills the young hopeful's apartment is seldom broken by the ringing of a phone that announces a Big Chance.

Generally, young hopefuls find themselves caught up in a society which flutters like butterflies around the important Hollywood people. His face is only one face in a crowd of eager, anxious faces begging for a chance to prove themselves. He eats, drinks, and breathes show-business. He gets sick of the diet when it seems to be getting him nowhere. He socializes with other struggling young People. If he is lucky, if he has talent, if he has worked hard and made the proper contacts, if he

7

has interested the right people, his chance will come and perhaps he'll move up into stardom.

The business of making pictures is handled by human beings who are, in many ways, no different than people in other businesses. It's a hard demanding business, where the competition is ready to do anything to beat you to the ground. The people with money are interested in making more money. Frequently they don't care about art or creative perfection. Perfection to them is an investment where each dollar invested returns two or more dollars.

When you become a star and have the world at your feet, you are babied and coddled, fawned over and pampered. All this attention does many things to a person. It is little wonder that a Liz Taylor can't find marital happiness after being the center of so much attention since childhood. Her marriages and divorces are to be pitied rather than criticized. A successful marriage in Hollywood is the exception, not the rule. Not only is a person's personal life up for grabs, but the temptations are super-human. What man would find it difficult to fall under the charm of some of the Hollywood queens? What woman could resist the attention of the Hollywood kings? Is it any wonder that they seek escape in drinking, in wild living and loving?

How horrible it must be to find yourself a universal sex symbol, the idol of every male in the world, and at the same time a failure in your own personal sexual relations.

Being a star has its frustrations. While having virtually everything, the human being discovers that fame doesn't bring complete happiness, or guarantee a successful marriage. They have what so many would give anything to possess, yet having achieved it, the realization that money and position does not provide true success and happiness can prove shattering.

The old Star system is long gone. The studios and production companies are run by business men and banks. The creation of movies is as cold and hard as a bank vault. The lucky actor or actress, today, finds himself the star of a television series. If the series is successful, and if he has a sharp agent and manager who will get him a percentage of the series or possibly even a controlling interest in the production company, he will work from sunup to sunset, and sometimes until all hours

8

of the night, six and seven day's a week, year in and year out.

When movies first began, Hollywood was only a name, and then it was a movie colony in the middle of nowhere. Slowly, the town grew with the Industry. The big studios like MGM, Warner, Fox signed talented young hopefuls to standard contracts, took control of their lives, developed and promoted them into stars. They were slaves to the system.

Hollywood became the movie capitol of the world and held that position until television sent a shock wave through the town and Industry which is felt even today. Only in later decades did these to elements mate and even marry at times. Today you have producers famous for their television series and even more famous for the major films! The crossover has become universal for the super giants. Jerry Bruckheimer's name comes swiftly to mind, for today he's one of the biggest crossovers around, as is J. J. Abrams who has moved from such hit shows as *Alias* and *Lost* to the making of major films in the early twenty-first century.

But previously, Hollywood went through its phases, it growing pains, from silent films to talkies, to television. With each phase new stars were born, new images created.

Before the present-day rating system there was the Hays Office, which for decades sat like a cobra waiting to strike any questionable morality, on or off film. For in the beginning, Hollywood *was* a true, wide-open city of immorality. There were the heroin dens, there were the wild parties and orgies given by people like Fatty Arbuckle.

Then three major things happened.

The Fatty Arbuckle trials, the death of Wallace Reid from an overdose of narcotics, and the murder of William Desmond Taylor brought to the public attention the very real and hard realities concerning the Industry.

At this point Will Hays was brought into the Hollywood society and his job was to clean up the public image of Hollywood, and to stop any scandals before they got started.

Then came the talkies and the new exciting phase of motion picture making. Hollywood was accepted as one of the most glamorous cities in the world. The giants were created, and Clark Gable, Lana Turner, Jean Harlow, Bette Davis, Errol

Flynn, became better known than the names of national political figures. The scandals in which Flynn became involved, his love affairs, created a term that many people now so fully accept that they don't even connect it with the actor: *"in like Flynn."*

There were other scandals to hit Hollywood, but the town was ready and able to handle them. Flynn was accused of seducing girls who were underage, and the trials were a sensation. Lana Turner's daughter, Cheryl Crane, was accused of having stabbed her mother's lover—but the whisperings were that the mother and not the daughter wielded the weapon. Rumors, rumors and more rumors, never the truth, just exciting stories to hear about, read about and to believe. After all, why should these Big Named People get all the breaks? They were rich, famous. Did they have to be happy, too?

Ingrid Bergman flaunted social custom and had her illegitimate child. Shocking, shocking! And today almost "common" in modern society! Liz Taylor's marriages became a laughing stock. Today marriage is less popular and living together is a norm for a large slice of the population. Marilyn Monroe was found dead from an overdose of sleeping pills.

Oh, how lovely it all is! And it ain't getting' no better!

What the future holds is anybody's guess. Someday another scandal will rock Hollywood, another star will suddenly become the center of world attention and another career will go down the drain.

Well, murder and death and drugs have managed to remain somewhat popular in their various forms. A mystery is always enjoyed. Even an accident, killing a popular English princess, will be mocked into some kind of tragic murder plot.

In this book we have presented some of the most shocking cases to hit the town in its early years, the most puzzling mysteries to come out of Hollywood. These were events that had major effects on how the town and industry was thought of worldwide and even by its own power brokers. And the following questions will be examined.

Was Fatty Arbuckle a sexual degenerate who took a young woman into a bedroom, raped her, then assaulted her body in a perverted way with a chunk of ice?

Was Paul Bern a degenerate homosexual, a sadistic ani-

10

mal, or a frustrated pitiful example of a man? Was he responsible for the death of Jean Harlow?

Was Lana Turner really a tramp; a woman who sold her daughter down the drain to protect her own hide?

Did Marilyn Monroe kill herself because life was passing her by? Had she failed in everything important in life, men, sex and career? And what about that D.C. connection?

Was William Desmond Taylor killed by a jealous lover or by a representative of the Chinatown heroin ring?

In almost every case, it was Hollywood, the town, the glitter and fame that destroyed each of these people. Without the fame, without the money and position, none of them would have become involved in scandal, murder or perversion.

The picture and story of Hollywood is still a living and growing thing. There are thousands of young people flocking to the city with glittering dreams in their eyes, begging the town to reach out and claw their souls naked. They will pay any price for fame and fortune, and the price might be too high.

It has never changed insofar as the human side, the normal cravings and driving hungers that force people down pathways all too tempting to ignore—and far too dangerous to embrace. Life in the fast lane is still dangers. And the telling and re-telling of these early scandals are still valid for they offer lessons others, today and tomorrow, are wise to learn and remember.

The following are just some of the Hollywood Mysteries that have never been resolved, and they will continue to hold their secrets and tempt the minds of the public for years to come.

I have somewhat updated the book since its original writing and publication in order to make it even more valid for today's readers.

—CHARLES NUETZEL
Thousand Oaks, California
July 2006

ABOUT THE AUTHOR

Charles Nuetzel was born in San Francisco in 1934, and writes:

"As long as I can remember I wanted to be a writer. It was a dream I never thought would materialize. But with the help of Forrest J Ackerman, who became my agent, I managed to finally make it into print.

"I was lucky enough not only in selling my work to publishers but also ending up packaging books for some of them, and finally becoming a 'publisher' much like those who had bought my first novels. From there it as a simple leap to editing not only a sci-fi anthology, but a line of sci-fi books for Powell Sci-Fi back in the 1960s. Throughout these active professional years I had the chance to design some covers and do graphic cover layouts for pocket books & magazines."

Much of his work in covers and graphics are a result of having had a father who was a professional commercial artist, and who did a number of covers for sci-fi magazines in the 1950s and later for pocket books—even for some of Mr. Nuetzel's books.

In retirement he has become involved in swing dancing, a long time lover of Big Band jazz. But more interestingly world travels have taken him (and his wife Brigitte) across the world, to Hawaii, Caribbean, Mexico, Kenya, Egypt, Peru, having a life-long interest in ancient civilizations. His website is full of thousands of pictures taken during these trips.

PART ONE

THE FATTY ARBUCKLE RAPE CASE

One wonders what cable television news would do with the following story. The media would have a great time, all channels blasting away at this new, juicy sex scandal involving a famous and beloved Hollywood comic and murder.

Like all famous stories involving Hollywood, then and now, the events reported about the Fatty Arbuckle rape case were mixed and cruel and damaging of his the reputation and career. The media cares little about people they report on, just so it makes a good story. What "facts" are actually reported against what actually happened are too many times counter to reality. Generally those involved are too invested in the outcome rather than the truth and justice. The Hollywood PR machines conflicted with the media's desire to "know." The public is willing to buy any juicy twist and turn that reveals the nasty underbelly of fame, fortune and the price paid by those lucky enough to be successful.

Twenty minutes after Roscoe "Fatty" Arbuckle disappeared into the bedroom with Virginia Rappe there was a long, high pitched scream. It was a scream which would haunt the famous silent movie comic for the rest of his life.

Four days after the scream, Virginia Rappe was dead. A short time later Fatty Arbuckle was taken into custody and charged with murder.

It was the "Roaring '20s" and Prohibition was in full swing. Hollywood had finally become a town of national importance, producing an endless supply of motion pictures, making unknowns more famous than kings and queens. Hollywood stars were loved and adored, worshipped, and anything they did was featured material for the national newspapers. A scandal concerning a motion picture star drew more attention than national elections.

Fatty Arbuckle was one of the most beloved of Hollywood personalities.

The minute Fatty was arrested, the newspapers were filled with the rape case. During the months following his arrest, it was to be established that Arbuckle had had sexual relations with Virginia and in the process her bladder had been ruptured. Rumors claimed that he had used either a bottle or a chunk of ice on the woman in a perverted way.

What actually happened between Fatty Arbuckle and Virginia Rappe could never be completely established, since they were the only ones who really knew the truth. She was dead and he was, for obvious reasons, admitting nothing.

After eight months of trials, though finally acquitted, Fatty Arbuckle found it impossible to return to the films. Public opinion was strongly set against him. Fatty was never able to completely shake off the effects of the scandal, though many personal friends and the high powers in Hollywood and show business did everything they could to help him.

Some years later, in New York, under the insistence of his friends, Fatty did a play called *Baby Mine,* which was highly successful. New York was sophisticated enough to accept his talent and not judge the man—but when he went across country on a stage tour, his appearances in Minneapolis were cancelled because of public and civic pressure. This was seven years after the trials.

Fatty went back to Hollywood to open a night club called *The Plantation Club.* Here in the city which had made him a national motion picture star he found it possible to obtain some kind of success in this business enterprise. When the depression came, the club had to close.

A short time later, in Palm Springs, Fatty received a call from Jack Warner who wanted him to make several comedy shorts. It was believed that enough time had passed since the rape scandal to take a chance on Fatty. After having finished the first short, Fatty went to New York with his third wife, and on April 29, 1933, died in his sleep, some twelve years after the scandal which had rocked Hollywood and the nation.

Until his fatal meeting with Virginia Rappe in the St. Francis Hotel in San Francisco, Fatty Arbuckle had been loved and adored by the public. Four days later he was finished as a movie actor. Such is the effect of scandal. To this day no one truly knows for certain if he had been falsely accused, a victim of circumstances, or if he had in fact brutally assaulted a young healthy woman, causing her death through a sadistic act of perversion. All that is known is his career was demolished over night!

Virginia Rappe was born in 1896 in Chicago. The career which would lead to her final destiny with Fatty Arbuckle began at an early age. At sixteen, she was working as an artists' model, already having developed into an extremely attractive young woman with an excellent figure. She was the type of girl who, even at this early age, showed a strong sense of independence. Because of her good looks and magnetic personality, she was able to snub her nose at social convention. A natural free spirit.

Her first serious romance involved a forty-year-old sculptor.

She was seventeen.

This affair came to a tragic end when, shortly after they'd become engaged, the man jumped off the roof of an apartment house. What changes might have been made in her life if the man hadn't committed suicide can never be calculated. But probably she'd never have become a plaything for the movie comic.

So the story goes.

Soon after the sculptor's death, Virginia studied dress designing and promptly started to make a reputation for herself in the field. At twenty-one she left Chicago and lived with an aunt in San Francisco. Fate was already beginning to play its hand in directing her toward the St. Francis Hotel. She fell in love again. This time she made an excellent choice. Robert Moscovitz's family was not only rich but they were also among the San Francisco elite. As a result of a childhood accident,

Robert had lost the use of one arm. This romance also came to a quick and tragic end when they were riding in a trolley car that became involved in an accident that took Robert's life.

Virginia moved to Los Angeles to forget the loss she'd suffered and under a doctor's advice she left the dress designing business in the hopes that she would be able to forget her past experiences which were so closely connected with this career.

Her first contact with the Hollywood industry came when she met a man named Irving Lehrman at a War Bond party, in 1917. As a well-established Hollywood director, Lehrman was in a position to not only see possibilities in Virginia as an actress, but he was able to do something about it.

In the months following, Virginia and Lehrman dated heavily, and with his help she met the important people in the Industry. He not only introduced her, but saw to it that she went out with those who would help promote her career. There is some question as to how willing and cooperative a date she was. During the trials which followed her death, the lawyers tried to build a picture of a woman who was loose and fast, willing to sleep with any man. If she were in fact sleeping with some of these very important Hollywood contacts—and certainly Lehrman would have been aware of this—then it seems strange that her romance with the director could have become so serious. Though it is seldom that a young woman will get very far in any business—especially in Hollywood—without pleasing the right people, it takes only one powerful contact, and Lehrman seemed to be hers. Their relationship gave every indication that she was more than simply holding hands with him. It is hardly believable that Virginia thought it necessary to freely offer herself to other men. If she had, it would have been merely the action of a passionate woman who flaunted convention and enjoyed sexual relations. It has been suggested that possibly Virginia was nothing more than a woman willing to sleep with the right person at the right time, and not a tramp.

Her relationship with Lehrman was more than casual, and finally developed into an engagement.

Her first picture was *Fantasy,* directed by her *fiancé.*

Virginia met Fatty Arbuckle when she went to visit Lehrman on the set of *Joey Loses a Sweetheart* in which the comic was starring. It was 1918 and Virginia had the reputation of being the "Best Dressed Girl in Pictures." Her experience in the dress designing business provided her with an advantage which other actresses didn't have—and with her attractive body, it isn't hard to understand why Fatty was impressed and expressed interest in getting to know her.

That night, Fatty, Virginia and Irving Lehrman went out to dinner together, with Arbuckle paying the bills in an attempt to impress the young actress. Her first important impression of the comic was made while they danced. Lehrman laughed off her complaint that Arbuckle had been a little too free with his hands. Virginia was angry and insisted that Fatty had been "fresh." The fact that this annoyed her seems to indicate that this first meeting was the beginning of what friends called Virginia's distaste for the comedian.

Virginia was selected to pose for the cover of the sheet music publication of *"Let Me Call You Sweet-Heart."* The event certainly served to give her national publicity. This event also gave Fatty a chance to impress Virginia by giving a celebration party in her honor. For the occasion, he hired several famous singers to sing the song to Virginia. This time, when Fatty danced with her, he managed to make a better impression. It isn't hard to understand that she was flattered and pleased by the attention that was centered around her because of this party.

Though she still wasn't won over completely, Virginia was said to have admitted that her first impression of Arbuckle might have been hasty.

Fatty was even more impressed with Virginia and made no secret about his interest in her. She was one of the few girls who didn't do everything to play up to him. He was determined to win her over and was no doubt willing to go to great lengths to eventually get her into a bedroom party.

Arbuckle's attempts to win Virginia included an offer of a co-starring role. Arbuckle sent his offer with a gold wrist-watch. The watch she kept.

The part she refused because she wanted to advance her career on her own and felt that taking advantage of the Arbuckle fame would, at least in her own mind, leave a question as to what had actually been responsible for "overnight" success.

The offer to star in *Twilight Baby* was accomplished without the help of either Fatty or Lehrman. Up to now, she had been limited to small parts, and when she was picked for this starring role her excitement knew no bounds. She was walking on air for days.

As Virginia's career advanced the relationship with Lehrman began to deteriorate. Exactly what caused their personal difficulties is hard to tell, but it is easy to guess that her career was now assured, the strong independence which had been a part of her personality since her middle teens asserted itself. There is some question about the depth of Lehrman's affection for Virginia, considering the fact he paid much attention to another woman during a studio party. Her own feelings for the director are hardly questionable for she was continuously pushing for a marriage, which Lehrman kept side-stepping. On September 1, 1921, the lid blew off when she insisted they get married. Lehrman refused, saying he wasn't making enough money to support a wife properly. The fact that Virginia was making $1,500 a week didn't count. Lehrman did not want to live on her income.

The argument which followed their discussion of marriage almost finished them then and there, but they finally made up. An event which took place the following day became directly responsible for what was soon to happen on the coming Labor Day, in San Francisco.

The couple went shopping for a birthday present which Lehrman wanted to give Wallace Reid. The gift was a very expensive ring which had a tiger-eye stone circled by diamonds. An argument started because Virginia couldn't understand how Lehrman could afford such a gift in light of what he'd stated about his financial condition. When the ring was bought, Virginia walked out of the shop and went home in a taxi.

Lehrman sent a note of apology to Virginia the next day and informed her that he was going on a business trip to New York. Virginia's first outward reaction was one of relief, because it would give her time to seriously consider the future possibilities of marriage with Lehrman. Later that day her emotions revealed a completely different response and it became necessary to cut short the day's shooting.

With a long Labor Day weekend before her Virginia was ripe for a suggestion to go on a trip—anything to keep her from facing long days in loneliness.

It was the girl friend of Virginia's personal manager, Al Seminacher, who was responsible for inviting her to San Francisco. Maude was going to spend the weekend in Fresno with Al, but when she met Fatty Arbuckle in a drug store—where she'd gone to buy a few items to take along with her—the plans were changed.

Fatty had decided to spend the holidays in San Francisco and suggested that Maude and Al come up there with her and that they should bring Virginia. He gave Maude $200 for her and Virginia. Maude doubted that Virginia would come if she knew Fatty was going to be there so she didn't mention it to her.

Virginia, Maude and Al went up in one car, and Fatty went up in another car. During the trip, Al had to stop five times along the way because Virginia wanted to go to the ladies' room.

This was a point which was brought out later in the trials because of its implication that she was having bladder trouble. It was a good argument for the defense whose case was hinged on the fact that Virginia wasn't in good health and that her bladder broke for the simple reason that it was already damaged, and not because of something Fatty had done to her.

They stayed at the Palace Hotel, a place which Fatty had suggested. Fatty went to the St. Francis Hotel where he was given a three-room suite—the best in the house. According to reports he was in a mood for an all-out good time with plenty of girls. Upon arriving, he immediately contacted a bootlegger in town and had a supply of booze brought to his rooms. The party was said to have started shortly after he'd arrived and continued around the clock. Monday morning he called the Palace Hotel. He hoped Al and Maude would talk Virginia into coming to the party.

There is little question that Fatty believed that now he had a good chance of winning Virginia and he was determined to make the most of it. He had been chasing girls since he'd reached adulthood and since becoming a star he had managed to have his pick. Virginia was one of the few who refused his attentions. His later actions would indicate that the intense desire he showed for Virginia was caused by her cold reaction to his advances.

Fatty didn't consider a woman's feelings. What he wanted, he went after. Once he would get what he was after, his interest faded. This habit of using women stemmed far back, and included his estranged wife, Minta. His reputation as a girl chaser had brought on the marital separation. The temptations of popularity and power had been too great for a man who for years had been unattractive to the opposite sex. As a teenager he had shown no outward interest in women. His heavy weight gave him an inferiority complex.

Fatty was born in the late 1880s in Kansas. He was a heavy child even at birth, weighing sixteen pounds. He started in show business in San Jose at the age of eight. Vaudeville was wide open in that time and Fatty got his groundwork in the entertainment business by working on the stage before its demanding audiences.

He was not only a heavy eater at an early age, but a heavy drinker. By the time he was at the peak of his career he was earning $5000 a week making pictures for Joseph Schenck Productions. He appeared in about one hundred two-reel comedies and almost forty feature length pictures. It was the pictures he made with Mabel Normand that made him famous almost overnight.

He married Minta when he was twenty-one. She was a young attractive girl of seventeen, and she stuck with him through the difficult years until he showed signs of being unable to resist all the young girls who flocked around him. He paid Minta $500 a month to stay out of his personal life. Though they were still good friends, it became impossible for Minta to put up with his running around and the separation had been the only solution.

He not only owned a custom-built car which had cost him $25,000, but also had five more for general use. His home was worth $250,000 and he lived there with only one servant. He was the kind of star who lived up to the image which the public expected of their Hollywood heroes. But more than that, he lived in a style which pleased himself. As one of the leading comics he was usually able to have his pick of the young ladies that flocked to Hollywood with stars in their eyes. Even the more established actresses didn't ignore what he could do for their careers if they played up to him.

Fatty didn't seem to mind—or possibly didn't allow himself to admit—that much of his charm and attractiveness was what he was able to do for a girl who pleased him. Virginia Rappe's open snubbing of his passes had made her even more desirable.

He was, nevertheless, well liked by much of the Hollywood crowd, and he was in a habit of giving out expensive presents to those who worked with him—as when he had given Virginia Rappe the gold wrist watch.

His insatiable desire for women trapped him in a chain of events which started with his call to the Palace Hotel, in the attempt to get Virginia Rappe to join his party.

It was Monday, September 5, 1921, and he hadn't slept since Saturday night. Alcohol had made his eyes bloodshot and his face bloated. By nine in the morning, he was the only one really alive in the hotel suite. Others were already too far under the effects of exhaustion and liquor to care much about anything. A San Francisco show girl by the name of Zey Prevon, who had become one of the guests, heard him complain, *"This is one hell of a party."* Three others, besides herself, were scattered around the room in different stages of drunkenness and sleep. Many bottles of bootleg booze were on the bridge table which had been set up as a bar.

After having a stiff drink, Fatty called the Palace Hotel and when he got Al Seminacher on the phone he started putting on the pressure to get Virginia and Maude over so that the party could be brought to life with new talent. He was in a bad humor and didn't make any attempts to be subtle as to what he wanted.

Al told Fatty that he couldn't promise to get Virginia to come over, but that he would do his best.

Al, for his part, went to Maude and pressed her into trying to talk Virginia into going to the Arbuckle party. Both of them were anxious to please the comic, recognizing his power and influence in Hollywood. Arbuckle was obviously in a bad mood, and if Virginia didn't show up Al was worried that Fatty would do something drastic.

Maude went into the hotel room she shared with the other actress and told Virginia—who was in the process of doing her morning exercises—that they'd been invited to a party, not mentioning who the host was by name.

When Virginia showed signs of reluctance and wanted to know who was doing the inviting, Maude acted as if she didn't know who was giving the party or who would be there. She suggested that they might go over and see, and if they didn't like the party, they would leave and go shopping.

On the way to the St. Francis, Virginia was more interested in the idea of shopping than going to a party and it took all the combined arguments of both Maude and Al to talk her into going. She finally agreed to look in and see how things were—if nothing interesting was happening they would leave.

In the meantime, Arbuckle had ordered food and shaved, but hadn't gotten out of the pajamas which he'd been wearing for some time. The room had been straightened up some and the player was alive with a Russ Columbo record.

Lowell Sherman was the man who answered the door at 11:45, the time of Virginia's arrival. He introduced himself and the trio entered, with Maude in front and Al last in line.

Lowell and Virginia had known each other before and everything seemed to be fairly friendly until Fatty suddenly turned from the window, which he had been opening, and greeted his guests. They were the first of a long line which had been invited, and before the party was over there would be thirty people who had been in and out of the hotel suite at one time or another.

Fatty was enthusiastic when he saw Virginia, but she was formal and distant. As she sat down and took off her shoes, which had been bothering her since leaving their hotel room, Fatty quickly offered a round of drinks. Virginia didn't immediately accept, but after some heavy urging from the host she finally asked for a Screwdriver—which was spiked with gin, rather than vodka.

Fatty, wanting to make a good impression on Virginia, offered a toast to her, and then took a large swallow of his own drink. Virginia merely sipped hers.

A bellboy arrived about this time with hors d'oeuvres.

Things started to liven up, Dollie, one of the other female guests, was showing off a dance step to Al. Other guests began arriving, and drinks were being passed around as soon as anybody was in need of a refill. A bit later, Dollie got into a conversation with Virginia and Fatty butted in long enough to pressure his number one mark for the day into finishing her drink. He was doing everything in his power to get her loaded enough so that things could become friendlier between the two of them.

Virginia announced that she didn't plan on staying long because she had a script at the Palace Hotel to study.

As new couples arrived, the party became a series of individual conversation groups.

The bathroom had been loaded with the major supply of liquor, which made it a very popular place.

Maude complained of a headache and Sherman, who claimed to have a good remedy for it, took her into the bathroom. The door was left half open and as Maude started to leave, with a glass of tomato juice—the remedy—a man by the name of Fishback crashed into the door, knocking the tomato juice over Maude's dress. Fishback's wife insisted on immediately cleaning the dress, saying that in less than half an hour it would be as good as new. It was this unpredictable incident which made it necessary for Virginia to stay the additional length of time which led to the fateful episode with Fatty in the bedroom.

Arbuckle urged Virginia to have something more to drink, but she refused and asked for some food and coffee. When Fatty promptly filled her "order," Virginia showed signs of surprise. Obviously this didn't seem like the kind of play a man might act out if he was trying to seduce a woman with liquor. This reaction was noticed by Fatty, and he was quoted as having told her he was only pushing drinks because *"I'm a good host."*

More people arrived and Arbuckle joked about his heavy weight. Everybody seemed to be having fun except Virginia who wanted to leave as soon as possible. She didn't care about drinking and cared even less about the party and Fatty. She asked Maude about the dress, but the other woman was a little high from the drinks and said she wasn't in any hurry. Maude parted the robe she'd been wearing, showing that there was only bra and panties on underneath.

Al had brought over a drink for Virginia and although she took it she announced that she hadn't ordered it.

A little after 2:00 p.m. a young actress by the name of Betty Campbell arrived. She was wearing a low-cut dress which revealed a goodly portion of her attractive body. The dress was important later because it apparently made an impression on Lowell Sherman for she accused the man of having made passes at her in the bathroom. If the passes were completed or not wasn't the issue, but this does bring out the point as to what type of party it was.

The fact that Betty had been in a picture with Virginia caused the woman to start a conversation with her. Virginia sipped her second drink during the conversation, so there is some indication that the actress was beginning to relax a little, possibly even beginning to feel her drinks.

Maude was highly under the influence of the alcohol and didn't seem to mind the fact that her robe was hanging free around her partly naked body.

Arbuckle had received the order for Virginia's food but managed to put it in the bathroom in a sly attempt to keep her occupied with drinking. Virginia was sitting on the floor now because her foot bothered her. She continued to sip the drink and talk to Betty.

The party at this time was given a sharp jolt of excitement by Maude's announcement that she was going to liven it up. Then she turned the radio higher and started doing her rendition of a Turkish harem dance that was meant to catch the eyes of all the men in the crowd. She had changed into a pair of Fatty's pajamas and when the dance was over her body was covered with perspiration. She announced that it was hot and unbuttoned the pajama top, which revealed that she now had nothing underneath. Fatty grabbed her and the two started dancing until somebody started encouraging him to take Maude's pajama bottoms off.

Virginia got a kick out of Maude's antics and finished her drink and began working on Betty's gin which the other woman hadn't touched. She was finally beginning to enjoy herself. Things then started moving fast. Another girl joined Maude and a jealous argument started between the two women about who had the most attractive breasts, an argument which couldn't be settled in a ladylike fashion. Maude tore at the girl's blouse, almost ripping it off. An all out catfight was in the offing and Fatty tried to stop it. In the struggles the show girl's bra was taken off and she was quick to point out the well-formed development of her breasts, a display which drove Maude into stepping out of the pajama bottoms. Somebody suggested that things had gone too far and that Maude should go get dressed before there was any chance of the law finding out what was going on. Maude, angered and in the mood to show off, started to pull down her panties but a man slapped her. She slapped back. It could have turned into an all-out fight, if the others hadn't broken it up.

Virginia complained to Betty that she had to go to the bathroom, but believed there was somebody already in there sick. Betty checked and announced that Virginia was right.

When Al heard about the woman in the bathroom he commented that he wasn't feeling too good either, that it must be the bootleg booze. Virginia asked if there was anything wrong with the liquor because she wasn't feeling well, either.

When the sick girl came out of the bathroom, Virginia got up but a man got there first. She announced that she would wait by the door until the man left the room.

Fatty, who had been involved with Maude, apparently affected by her display a few moments before, suddenly left the woman and went after Virginia.

There is some confusion as to what happened next. The majority of those still at the party—over twenty witnesses—said Arbuckle intercepted Virginia, took her hand and announced in a loud voice that this was what he'd been waiting to have for five years, then ushered her into the bedroom. Virginia didn't struggle or show any signs that she wasn't a completely willing partner in this new development. She went into the bedroom first. Fatty winked to those behind him, and then followed Virginia, closing and locking the door.

The points which were brought out in the trials concerning this move was that Virginia didn't make any sign of struggle or objection. This was a strong argument for the defense, in that it pointed out that whatever happened in the locked room was apparently not against the girl's will.

But the trials made an issue of a statement made by one of the witnesses, to the effect that Virginia walked like a person who was dazed, as if hypnotized. She was on her way to the bathroom, had been anxious to relieve herself, a sure indication that her bladder was in a condition which might cause it to be easily ruptured.

The fact remains that they were in the room for twenty minutes, a long enough time for Fatty to have had relations with her at least once, and possibly twice, according to witnesses and medical reports.

The mystery in part lies in the fact that nobody ever really knew what her mental condition was when she went into the room with Fatty. Possibly she did know what was happening, and wasn't as much against Fatty as she'd let on. Maybe she had some vague idea that by allowing such a thing to take place it would make Irving Lehrman jealous.

Nobody in the outer room really knew what actually went on in the bedroom. Fatty never told the same story twice—except on the witness chair.

Possibly the liquor had excited her, maybe the combination of liquor, the dancing and the nudity which had been a part of the party was responsible for a change in her attitude.

The theory was that Fatty, having once possessed Virginia, had used a coke bottle or chunk of ice in a sadistic and perverted way on her body. Supposedly this was responsible for the damage done internally to her. And this was later widely circulated during the trials. A media dream bite! Fat man kills lady with a bottle! Comic pervert seduces with a hard chunk of ice! What headlines it would make even today! The tabloids would run wild! Even then the newspapers reported their version and conclusions to end Arbuckle's career, uncaring about the true facts. The public's frenzy for juiced up insight into the perversions of the rich & famous had to be feed! And the newspaper well was bloody with half-truths and wild conclusions meant to bait readers into continually buying the papers in which they were printed. To say nothing about radio reports churning the airways.

Regardless of how it happened in that hotel room that day, the first indication that something was wrong took place twenty minutes later when those outside heard a loud scream of agony, then silence.

Maude tried to get Fatty to open the door and let her in, but there was no sound except a low moan which slowly began to gain in volume. The moan was not one of passion. Maude began to get frightened and hit the door with her slipper. But whatever Fatty was doing he didn't stop. The moaning continued. Then suddenly, it was reported, Virginia screamed again and yelled. *"He's killing me!"*

Zey Prevon went to Maude's side and the women tried to get Fatty to open the door. Finally Maude went to the house phone and called the desk. In a short time the assistant manager appeared, and after being told what was happening knocked on the door, demanding that Arbuckle open it.

After a short silence, the door opened and Fatty stood there. His face and body, naked from waist up, was covered with perspiration. Apparently he made some attempt to look casual, for he looked toward Virginia, who was lying on the bed, saying that she'd be all right, and that she was only drunk.

The assistant manager, Maude and Zey found Virginia twisted in agony, clawing at her abdomen. They later said she moaned. *"I can't breath. Help me!"*

Though at one time it was claimed that Virginia didn't have anything on, later nobody was sure, or at least refused to admit it one way or another. Her clothing disappeared shortly wards.

Virginia, herself, apparently claimed before she died that Arbuckle had raped her.

A doctor was called, but his examination didn't go far enough to reveal that there was any trouble with Virginia's bladder. He merely accepted the fact that she was drunk, and that this was responsible for her condition. He said that Virginia should be given plenty of rest. Before he had arrived, Maude and Zey tried several means of helping the hurt girl. She was given a bicarbonate which she quickly threw up. Her moaning continued on and off for the next several hours.

Arbuckle was supposed to have yelled that if she didn't shut up he was going to throw her out the window. His coldness to her indicated that he didn't really care about the girl. Possibly he was reacting from fear and drunkenness himself. It is hard to imagine a man being so indifferent at a time like this.

The girls on the other hand were scared by the time the first doctor arrived. When he left Arbuckle announced that Virginia couldn't stay there, but that he would pay for another room to put her in. He complained it was because of her that the party was finished, and acted as if everything was her fault. His actions were, once again, those of a man who thought that women were only to be seduced, used and forgotten. Possibly he was angered because she'd somehow tried to fight him during intercourse. The fact that some claimed that her thighs were bruised would surely indicate that Fatty might have used force and her statement to the effect that he had raped her, seemed to back this up.

She was moved into another hotel room, by the girls and two men, while Arbuckle showed his complete lack of interest by showering.

Virginia was still moaning and in agony. She should have had an immediate operation. The fact that this first doctor didn't discover and treat her condition surely helped to kill her. She needed immediate surgical attention.

At Zey's suggestion she was given a cold bath. This was one of the worst things that could possibly be done to her. Virginia screamed when they lowered her into the water.

It was after drying the girl off that Maude decided they should get another doctor. She was now afraid for Virginia's life.

Since Arbuckle was involved, Zey went to him telling what they planned to do. He showed no sign of interest and made it clear that they could do what they wanted since he had more important things to consider.

When they were waiting for the second doctor to arrive, one of the girls thought of putting warm compresses on Virginia's abdomen, which turned out to be the best thing they could have done.

When Dr. Rummel arrived, he didn't need more than three minutes to realize the seriousness of Virginia's condition. He immediately instructed hospitalization and an operation for a ruptured bladder.

Virginia was taken to the Wakefield Sanatorium, arriving at eight p.m., some five hours after her first scream. Doctors claimed that this delay was responsible for her death.

Fatty was told about the new developments, but he still showed no sign of concern, except to say that he'd take care of the bills. With that, he made arrangements to leave for Los Angeles on the *California,* a steamer which in those days made the trip between the two cities. As far as Fatty was concerned, what had happened between Virginia and himself was not his responsibility. Possibly he felt himself generous in offering to pay the bills.

Virginia was operated on that night, but didn't awake until Wednesday at which time she was still on the critical list. A nurse by the name of Vera Cumberland claimed that Virginia accused Arbuckle of her condition, saying that she didn't want the man to get away with it. Virginia didn't seem to remember very much of the details but knew that Arbuckle had used her body.

Vera reported that Virginia was covered with nicks and bruises all the way down to her knees. The testimony of this witness supported the case against Fatty, and certainly presented a picture of a man who had taken a woman for his own base needs and used her, brutally, only to toss her aside afterwards without a care in the world.

By Friday, there was no hope for Virginia. She now had a case of peritonitis and there was nothing the doctors could do for her.

Maude sat by Virginia until the end.

She died at one p.m. on Friday of peritonitis, which had been caused as a direct result of the damage done to the bladder and the lateness of the operation, blame for which was to fall on Fatty Arbuckle's shoulders.

There is a good chance that Fatty Arbuckle would never have been brought to trial except for several events which brought the case to the attention of the Deputy Coroner of San Francisco.

There is reason to believe that though Arbuckle had shown no outward signs of interest in what happened to Virginia that he was possibly more concerned about her condition than he allowed it to be known.

It was believed at the time by many authorities that Virginia's condition at first was purposely kept from the press to keep any scandal from starting. A natural Hollywood PR trick; media muffling was a normal method of protecting stars. The studios couldn't afford to have highly invested products damaged by bad publicity. Fatty Arbuckle was a major investment for those who produced his films, backed his career. But the media had its own ax to grind away in the "public interest" and paper profits. Selling papers sold ads and ads meant money. Business was business. And the media knew exactly how to grind out the "news" in a manner attractive to the "unwashed" millions who bought their product.

One nurse reported that she was taken off the case because she'd talked to some reporters, though not about Virginia.

The actual event which attracted Coroner Michael Brown's attention was a phone call from the hospital. The woman asked when the autopsy was going to take place. Brown wanted to know what autopsy she was talking about. She started to explain but was suddenly cut off.

Interesting!

Brown called back, and when he got the woman on the phone he was informed that she didn't have any information to give him.

Even more interesting!

His reaction to this was to go out and investigate. He quickly discovered that a twenty-five-year-old woman had died that afternoon. Doctors, puzzled by her death, had performed an autopsy on their own. When Dr. Brown insisted on examining the vital organs and discovered that there was a ruptured bladder he demanded explanations. He had the police do some official investigation and it was soon revealed that the woman was Virginia Rappe. From then it became public news.

And *what* news!

Maude and Zey were more than willing to let the authorities and press know the full truth about what had happened to Virginia. At least their truth. Did it matter if this might conflict with the studio version? Or any version? Was it the truth or in some way colored? Did they have any reason to pervert their story? That seems unlikely. Yet what happened in the room there was not witnessed by anybody other than Fatty and Virginia—two people, one dead and the other certainly determined to protect himself. His version of the truth didn't seem to gel with other reported "facts."

On September 10, when Arbuckle arrived back in Hollywood, he was picked up outside his home by the San Francisco police, who told him he was wanted for questioning concerning the death of Virginia Rappe. They were polite but firm, giving him the chance to come voluntarily. Arbuckle had not learned about Virginia's serious condition and didn't expect this development. His shock and surprise must have been overwhelming, but if he had any feeling about his role in her death, his cooperation and statements to the officers revealed a complete lack of any sense of guilt.

When the police refused to tell him about how she died, Arbuckle was fast to say that if it had anything to do with what had happened in his hotel suite in San Francisco that he couldn't be held responsible because he'd never been with her alone for more than a few minutes.

The police were polite but still said that they wanted him to come to San Francisco for questioning. Arbuckle requested the right to call his lawyer, Frank Dominguez, who quickly said not to say anything until they'd had a chance to talk to each other in private.

On his arrival, Dominguez quickly informed the police officers that he would bring Fatty to San Francisco and hand over a written statement at that time.

At first Dominguez told Fatty that there was nothing to worry about and that in a couple of days the whole thing would be over.

What Dominguez didn't know was that the scandal which would follow, once the papers published the story, would make it impossible to escape a manslaughter charge.

At first, the San Francisco District Attorney wanted to charge Arbuckle with first degree murder, on the claim that the comic had actually brutally assaulted a normal healthy young woman who had died as a direct result of his sexual attack.

Dominguez was fully aware of what they could be up against the moment he had a chance of learning all the facts from Arbuckle. They were going into a strange city. There had been a rivalry between San Francisco and Los Angeles for years. As strange as this might seem today, it was a very strong point in that the San Francisco authorities believed it was time to bring an end to the wild goings on of Hollywood people who came to their city, and the Arbuckle case was to be made an example.

Interesting, considering now how things have changed. Today it might go the other way around, with Los Angeles pointing wagging fingers at "that town up there" as "gay city"! The coin has flipped for the wicked little minds of blue nosed moral bigots who just love damning those who live a different life-style from their own.

The written statement which Fatty Arbuckle handed the San Francisco authorities is as follows:

> I was alone in my suite having breakfast when some friends of mine and Miss Rappe came to visit me. Miss Rappe started to drink almost immediately. Shortly after she had a few drinks she became hysterical and complained that she couldn't breathe and started to tear at her clothes. I requested that two of the girls in the room take care of her. She was disrobed and placed in a bathtub to be revived. The immersion did not benefit her and I then telephoned the hotel manager, telling him what was wrong and

Miss Rappe was take to another room and put to bed. When there was no change in her condition a doctor was called. I was at no time alone with Miss Rappe. During this time in my rooms there were at least a half dozen people there all the time and I can produce witnesses to bear out this statement.

Whatever possessed Fatty Arbuckle to have written such a statement certainly can't be even guessed at. Possibly he didn't realize how seriously he was involved, or how many witnesses had already been questioned.

In police Captain Duncan Matheson's office in front of Chief of Police Daniel O'Brien, and the Assistant District Attorney, and in front of about fifteen newsmen and photographers, Fatty was charged with the first degree murder of Virginia Rappe. He was to be held without bail.

The long stunned silence which followed was finally broken when one photographer asked for a smile. Arbuckle, shaken by the unexpected blow, announced that this wasn't the time for smiling. When the newsmen asked for a statement, he refused to make any.

Arbuckle was immediately jailed. Although his attorney did what he could to get him out, nothing worked.

Two investigations were taking place at once on the Arbuckle case: the Grand Jury and the coroner's inquest. When the District Attorney, Matthew Brady took charge, things started to tighten up around Arbuckle. Brady was a highly regarded man and, it was suggested, out to "hang" the comic.

The announcement of Arbuckle's arrest was world wide headline news. What really made it hard for Fatty was the fact that this attack was being made not only on him but on Hollywood, which was labeled a town of sin and vice, wild living, populated by misfits and degenerates.

Hollywood had to consider *itself* before Fatty Arbuckle. It could either go all out in support of him—and go down the drain if Fatty were convicted—or denounce the comic and lose their investments in the many films which were still unreleased in which he starred. They hesitated making a stand either way.

And considering all the facts, before and later, one can't blame them. No matter which way they turned it was a no win! They were going to lose one way or the other. So, it was a matter of deciding which side of the coin was the least expensive to bet on.

Duncan Matheson, speaking for the authorities, was quoted in the papers as having said:

> This woman, without a doubt, died as a result of an attack by Arbuckle. That makes it first-degree murder without a doubt. We don't feel that a man like Arbuckle can pull stuff like this in San Francisco and get away with it.

And then the lid really blew off.

This statement was an open accusation against Hollywood. It implies that while maybe the police department in Los Angeles was willing to put up with the immoral antics of Hollywood society, the San Francisco police wouldn't.

Now either Hollywood denied all responsibility for Fatty, saying he was an exception, or they had to deny the charges and claim that Fatty was completely innocent and put forth all its resources to see that he got off, regardless of his guilt or innocence. Morality, truth, be damned! The town was now split as to which stand to take.

One of Arbuckle's staff of lawyers was quoted as saying:

> When a man steals, he sets out to break the law. When a man drives while drink he is in the process of breaking the law. But Roscoe Arbuckle set out to do no more than have sexual relations with a girl he had known for fire years. I'd guess that 1,000,000 men set out every night to try and do the same thing Arbuckle did— cohabit with a woman. What happened was an unfortunate accident. He was a victim of a cruel twist of fate. What purpose does punishing Arbuckle serve...? To be an example for men not to

have intercourse with women? Every man I talk to is guilty at one time or another of pressuring a girl into having intercourse with him. Yet he walks free. It was an unfortunate accident. He should be set free.

If it is true that Arbuckle didn't use any brutal force against Virginia, and that she died of a ruptured bladder merely by accident, and not because of some unnatural perversion, then the lawyer's statement is surely fair. Arbuckle was either being victimized by San Francisco police, or was justly charged with the brutal assault on a normal healthy woman.

The nurse from Wakefield Sanitarium, Martha Hamilton, told the Grand Jury that Miss Rappe had constantly asked her if they had caught Arbuckle or found out where he was hiding. She was *"under the delusion (partly induced by sedation) that Arbuckle was trying to elude the police and was trying to escape."*

Delusion or not, the fact that she felt the man should be hiding away from the police certainly would indicate a mental attitude that supported her statements that Arbuckle had raped her. At least, it implies that Virginia believed him responsible for her condition. A fact that strongly refutes Fatty's claim of innocence.

Of course, Virginia's words were being fed to the media through a third party. They may have been a "perfect recording" of the woman's statement. But no tape recorder was there to set it down. Only a nurse had heard and reported these words, and she may or may not have distorted the meaning, or pulled them out of content. After all, these may have been nothing more than the ramblings of a dying woman. Who may or may not have remembered events as they truly happened. Too many ifs. Too many unknowns. Too many possible distortions.

What went against Fatty Arbuckle more than anything else was the fact that the newspapers played the story up big, taking the sensational side of the events and exaggerating them:

HOLLYWOOD COMIC STAR TAKES YOUNG GIRL INTO BEDROOM AND RAPES HER!

They played with the rumor that he had used either a coke bottle or chunk of ice. This was damning, though it was never established as fact.

Oh. But what a lovely vision this version offered up. Fat man toying with lovely, beautiful, innocent starlet. Abusing her virginal body with bottles or ice. Not enough that he would rape her in a "normal" way but that he's murdered her in a terribly sadistic manner! How juicy could it possibly get?

When Virginia's outer clothing was found in a waste basket in Maude's closet, the papers really had a field day, even though she claimed to know nothing about them. The fact that the undergarments were missing seemed to imply that there was good reason for their disappearance.

Public opinion turned against Fatty to the point where his pictures were banned from major theaters, something which would finally be taken up by all theater owners. The very fact that the San Francisco police force believed they had enough evidence to convict Fatty of first degree murder was enough to convince the public that the comic was at least morally guilty.

If not down right disgustingly guilty of perversions against humanity.

At least against a pure, sweet, innocent young lady.

What if it had been your daughter?

Or your sister or wife?

Can we let this kind of thing happen?

Do we want this kind of monster walking the streets?

Worse of all, do we want this kind of model for your young boys to admire?

No!

Hang the man! Rip his heart out. Bring on the band and lynch him! Bring on the booze, food, and wild women and we'll party as his dancing feet are flying in the wind.

So much for mob violence and morality.

He'd been an example, in a way, to American society. Now, if he were able to get away with this bloody crime, then it would be a *very* bad example to the youth, teaching that they too could get away with any sexual crime. This was a ticklish situation. Not only was Hollywood involved, but now a wider range of implications suggested themselves.

What's even more frightening is the undercurrent, the unstated idea that, "is it even important that he is guilty or not" the lesson to our children must be made, even if he is innocent of this crime. He certainly is guilty of some crime, somewhere. After all, it was his party, held in a hotel room, with lots of illegal booze and wild women. A sex bash that perhaps was damning enough to ruin his career. Serve the man up as an example to the world. Let everybody know that no matter how famous, no matter how powerful and rich, "ya can't get away with it, baby!"

The moral outrage was ideal to sell papers! Or ads on radio. Profit was blistering dollar signs and morality lessons that went beyond mere guilt or innocence.

That was, no doubt, much of the media's rationality for hammering the nails into Arbuckle's hands, and stringing his career up on a moral cross of indignation.

But Hollywood still played it cautiously as it attempted to keep as distant from the case as possible. The vice-president of Paramount, Jesse Lasky, stuck his neck out only far enough to simply say, *"Every man is innocent until found guilty by a due process of court."* And though in a legal sense the man was right, the public thought differently and the banning of Fatty's films continued.

Fatty's fan mail included an endless sea of hate and threats against him, sent for the most part by women.

To make things worse, District Attorney Brady and Fatty's defense lawyer, Dominguez, began a personal attack on each other. The newspapers had another field day.

Brady was politically ambitious and possibly he was merely attempting to get a lot of publicity out of the situation. He certainly managed to make himself part of the Hollywood Fatty Arbuckle legend.

During the Grand Jury inquest, witnesses gave conflicting evidence.

Boyle, the assistant manager of the St. Francis Hotel, stated that he considered Fatty to be a kindly man, and that he believed that the man had been extremely kind to Virginia

Rappe. His testimony established that Fatty had taken on financial responsibility for the girl.

Maude Delmont stated that Fatty grabbed Miss Rappe by the hand and dragged her into the bedroom against her will. This statement was one of the turning points against Fatty during the questioning before the Grand Jury. If Maude was telling what she believed to be true or not is unimportant; what's important is that she said it, that she felt it should be said because she held Fatty directly responsible for Virginia's death.

Dr. Rummel, who had been asked by friends of Virginia to perform a postmortem on her body reported to the Grand Jury, *"I found that much internal damage had been done by some deplorable, rough treatment."*

The Grand Jury, upon hearing all the evidence, felt that a first degree murder indictment was out of line. Fatty Arbuckle was held on a manslaughter charge, which implied, accidental murder.

The fact that Fatty seemed to be highly self-centered in his sexual relations with a woman is supported by a statement by Maude who admitted having had an affair with Arbuckle. Maude claimed to understand how it was possible for Virginia's insides to have been torn by Fatty.

New York reporters contacted Irving Lehrman who was still in that town. They wanted to know his feeling and connections with Virginia. He told them:

> I've been all broken up. Haven't slept since it happened. I requested that burial be in Los Angeles because she loved the town so much and I want her near me. Arbuckle is guilty. I hate him and if I ever see him I'll kill him. My baby died game like a real woman. She fought him until she lay dying. He outraged her and you know she told her nurse not to tell me about it because she didn't want me to know. I loved her very much. You know, we were engaged...you know, Arbuckle was an ignorant man. He had too much money and too much success. Now I hope the law punishes him.

This display of love and hate connected with Virginia's death could have been an honest statement as to his feelings, even though there was some questions whether the man ever meant to marry Virginia. He had also said:

> When I directed his pictures, I always had to warn him to stay out of the women's dressing rooms. As soon as he smelled perfume, he'd follow the stuff like a bird-dog. Arbuckle used to throw orgies and stag parties all the time. Thanks goodness I never attended one of his parties. A man like that ruins the reputation of a whole industry. I'm sure Virginia didn't know what kind of a party she was getting involved in or she would never have gone.

From the first trial on, the confusion started. Some witnesses disappeared, other witnesses changed their stories. Even Maude later announced that,

> I didn't exactly see Virginia and Arbuckle go into the bedroom but I saw him drag her to the door. No, she did not make an outcry.... When we came into the bedroom after Virginia had been screaming she was writhing on the bed. She had all her clothes on, even shoes and stockings, but not her panties and her dress was pulled up so that from the belly button down she was nude.

The nurse, Vera Cumberland, who had taken care of Virginia in the hospital claimed that the girl told her that Arbuckle had been a beast. Then she added: *"I was so hounded by Hollywood people to keep my mouth shut that I begged to be taken off the case. I was afraid."*

She stated that she had been threatened, but didn't name names.

Even Al Seminacher, Virginia's manager, refused to admit that he knew anything about what had really happened. He said that Virginia could not hold her liquor, that after a drink or two she was intoxicated

Even Zey began claiming that Virginia went into the room *"because she wanted to."* Then she refused to say more, after which the statement she had given the police soon after Virginia's death was read:

"When I walked into the room Virginia was writhing on the bed...she said to me, 'He killed me. Arbuckle did it.'"

When Arbuckle was officially charged with manslaughter on September 14, the coroner's jury announced:

> Miss Virginia Rappe unfortunately had sexual relations with Roscoe "Fatty" Arbuckle against her will. During those sexual relations such force was applied by Arbuckle that Miss Rappe was mortally hurt. We recommend such steps be taken that will prevent such outrages in San Francisco.

In the days that followed, District Attorney Brady started getting evidence that there had been payoffs made to get rid of witnesses or have them change their stories. Though he made public announcements accusing Hollywood of trying to suppress the Arbuckle case by attempting to get him off with big money, there was never any proof. Then Brady suddenly received excellent information to the effect that Fatty had, in fact, used unnatural means to assault Virginia Rappe. It came from Al Seminacher, who was fed several drinks to make him more willing to be communicative. C. A. Doran had questioned Al and reported that the man claimed Arbuckle had told him that *"he shoved a chunk of ice up Virginia and that is what caused all the trouble."*

This was later denied by Al, but the damage was done. Brady announced before the trials started that *"Virginia Rappe was raped, tortured, mangled and desecrated by that beast, and I'll prove it in court.*

Arbuckle, in the meantime, was freed on bail and on September 30th gave one of his biggest parties—though without liquor. Possibly, it was an escape from the horror of what now faced him. Arbuckle never showed any real concern over the fact that Virginia had died.

The key witness for the prosecution was Maude Delmont but they found that it was impossible to let her appear on the witness stand. She'd been involved in a bigamous marriage, and any testimony she might make would be discredited.

After all witnesses testified and "expert" medical testimony had been presented by both Brady and Fatty's trial lawyer, Arbuckle was brought to the stand and made this statement about what had happened during the party:

I had a few days off from film making and came to San Francisco for a rest. It has always been one of my favorite cities. I called a friend of mine, Mae Taubwe, and we decided some time during Labor Day I'd take her for a drink around the city. I shaved, put a robe over my pajamas and sat down to have breakfast with two of the boys who came to San Francisco with me. Then this one and that one started dropping in. Fred Fishbeck had borrowed my car and said he'd be right back. So while Mae was there we couldn't leave yet.

Well there were a few people in the room including Virginia Rappe who came in with some other people. Someone was playing the radio and someone was dancing, but it was quiet and orderly. Finally Fred came back and Mae suggested we go for that drive. I thought I was a good idea because it was warm and stuffy in my room. Well, I went out the bathroom to freshen up and dress and I had trouble opening the door. Virginia Rappe was on the floor of the bathroom and she as moaning in pain. She was leaning against the door so that I had to push gently in order to get into the bathroom.

I tried to talk to her but she was just moaning and I couldn't make out what was wrong with her. There were twin beds in my room and I put her on one of the beds. Then I went into the bathroom and continued with my preparations for the drive. After ten minutes later when I came out of the bathroom I saw Virginia wasn't on the bed where I had put her. I noticed she had fallen down between the two beds. I tried to pick her up but she was wedged there. I called Maude Delmont and Zey Prevon to help me. One of the hotel people, Mr. Boyle, was with them. We picked her up and got her on the bed again and called the hotel doctor. That's the whole story. There's nothing else to it.

The assistant D. A., Leo Friedman, asked Arbuckle how he accounted for the fact that so many witnesses, on both sides, had stated he had locked the bedroom door, that he was alone with Virginia at this time, and Fatty countered with, *"In order to freshen up and change I needed ten minutes of privacy. Miss Rappe was out on the bed. I opened the door again when I had prepared my toilet."*

Friedman stated that he had heard seven versions of the story of what happened which Fatty had told others. He wanted to know why, and Fatty simply claimed there was only one true story and that was the one he'd told just now in court.

After cross examining Fatty, using every means at his disposal, Friedman finally gave up trying to break down the man's story and suggested this one to be the truth:

Virginia Rappe had a few drinks and you lusted after her. You pulled her into the bedroom, locked the door, threw her on the bed despite her protestations, tore some of her clothes off and raped her a)td Lord knows what other perversion you practiced on a helpless girl who was at your mercy. When you tore her insides out and she screamed for mercy, you callously said you'd throw her out the window if she didn't shut up. That's the true story, isn't it, Mr. Arbuckle?

Fatty quietly denied it.

The fact that there had been many witnesses who claimed that Virginia had suffered from many attacks, especially after having a drink, which had caused her to react similarly to her actions in the hotel bedroom, coupled with Fatty's steadfast story that he'd never been responsible for having intercourse with the woman, caused Friedman to finally say:

> There's been a lot of nonsense about Virginia Rappe having had internal problems and pain, but not once have we heard from any doctor who treated Miss Rappe. You'd think a young girl with ample money and sophistication would see a doctor about such a serious problem. I'll tell you why we haven't seen proof of such medical examination.
>
> It's because this man ripped the insides of a perfectly healthy and normal girl with beastly passions.

During this first trial, the evidence on both sides was so confused and incomplete that when it went to the jury on December 2, it took over forty hours to come to the conclusion that it was impossible to decide upon a verdict. After forty-one hours, the Judge called a halt. He brought the jury back into the court and discharged them. During those hours it was believed that some seventeen ballots were made. The final ballot was reported to be ten to two.

The jury foreman said:

> Whether guilty or not the facts or evidence given by the prosecution were an insult to our intelligence. It was all conjecture—no facts, no proof. I was disgusted with them!

The only real holdout was a woman who had refused to budge her conviction that Fatty Arbuckle was a sexual degenerate.

Another juror believed Fatty guilty but felt the prosecution hadn't presented its case properly, and that if they had, the vote would have been unanimous for conviction.

Arbuckle felt that he had been morally acquitted, even if not legally acquitted. He stuck the story that he had merely tried to help Virginia and that he was a victim of circumstances. He was sure that the second trial would free him completely.

The second trial proved that either witnesses had been actually paid off or that they had in the time between forgotten some of the details. Zey's statement that she might have been wrong during the first trial certainly suggested a payoff. She also claimed that the San Francisco authorities had originally held her against her will until she made the kind of statement they wanted.

This kind of story was handed out by many of the witnesses. It was now getting to the point where both defense and prosecution were implying payoffs.

One magazine article pointed out that almost every major statement against Fatty made during the first trial was now either changed or contradicted, and to prove its point, made a listing of these contradictory statements.

When all the evidence had been handed in and the jury left to make its decision, Fatty stated that:

> My only fear is that there might be another hung jury. I know no jury on earth will call me guilty from what I've heard in this courtroom. If this jury can't reach a decision, a third trial would ruin me even if they acquit me. If there is a hung jury this time I will never be able to go back to the films again.

The things he said in this statement turned out to be all too true. There was a hung jury, the third trial did acquit him, and his career was ruined in pictures.

What actually threw out chances of an acquittal in this second trial was the fact that the defense counsel, Gavin McNab made the mistake of believing that it was unnecessary to make a strong argument. He told the jury: *"I think it would be silly at this time for me to repeat everything that has been said. I am sure the jurors are weary enough so I will waive my closing argument."* This mistaken belief that he had the case tied up this time was directly responsible for the ruin of Fatty Arbuckle's movie career.

Another long wait followed, while the jury argued among themselves. After the fourteenth ballot, which stood at nine to three for conviction, they were asked by the Judge if they would come to a decision. When the answer was no, the jury was excused, thus creating another hung jury.

The fact that the third trial, which ended some eight months after the Labor Day party, acquitted Fatty within six minutes after they had been excused indicated several things.

Either Fatty had been falsely accused and his story was the truth, and only public opinion had been responsible for the difficulty of getting him acquitted in the first two trials, or merely that time had played in his favor. The San Francisco authorities had fought hard during the first two trials, but were either up against too much Hollywood money—which had paid off witnesses—or they had actually been accusing an innocent man.

It was never claimed that Brady had sat down on the job. He'd done everything within his power to win the case and convict Fatty Arbuckle of a crime for which he truly believed the man responsible.

It was Sherman who was quoted as saying that the real reason that it wasn't possible to conclusively build a case on hard facts was because:

"Only Mr. Arbuckle knows what went on between him and Virginia in the bedroom. That wasn't for our eyes."

Fatty Arbuckle's career was ruined. During the trial William Desmond Taylor had been shot, a mystery which was never solved, Wallace Reid died of an overdose of narcotics, and the public was aware that Hollywood wasn't just a city of make-believe. The glamour capitol of the movie world was also a place where dope addiction, murder and rape were being played out in real life.

Some people claimed that Fatty was an innocent victim. His wife Minta always supported him, even though they had been separated for years. She stood by Fatty throughout the trials, and stated time and again to the papers that her husband was innocent; that he wasn't the kind of man who would do such a thing.

Possibly the truth is somewhere between the black and the white. Fatty Arbuckle, on the top of the world, a man who had never been very attractive to women but found it now possible to have almost any woman, found Virginia Rappe irresistible and took her into the hotel bedroom and had sexual intercourse with her. If he actually did perform some perverted means of sexual assault will never be known for sure. He was drunk, so was Virginia. The fact that Virginia had been on the way to the bathroom before having been urged by Fatty into the bedroom would certainly suggest that her bladder was in a weakened condition which contributed to its rupture. Why she went into the room with Fatty is a mystery. Being drunk, possibly she didn't know what she was doing. Her later statement to the fact that they had had relations, and that Fatty had raped her, is supported by witness reports as to what seemed to have happened and the medical statements as to the condition of her thighs.

But the only living witness was Fatty. And he claimed to be innocent.

Arbuckle might not have been responsible for the woman's weakened bladder, and he certainly didn't know of her condition, but his actions, afterwards, were not those of a gentleman who thought much about women.

Of course, morality, rules, whatever, are not all that important to the rich & powerful in any culture, in any state or nation. Powerful men used women as toys and playthings. It is more the norm to enjoy power over the opposite sex, be the person in power male or female. Power itself demands submission. Without using power to get your way, your wishes fulfilled, what's the use of having that power?

Today we are told that even huge international religions such as the Roman Catholic Church hides facts and evidence of perverse acts against children, protecting priests who are guilty of the worst possible crimes. They protect their own. But even these types of power plays are being fractured by a news media willing to look carefully at such self-protective systems. It runs down the line. No matter where you look, be it from religious right or left, or political right or left, or middle, the perversion of power and its seductive sway is evident on all levels. Too many of us human beings need to gain power to control others to our will. Luckily there is a counter balance. But even there, like the criminal courts, nothing is perfect. We see egos and careers rise and fall on the successful use of power. So what if somebody innocent is crushed into the cracks. Just so those in power succeed, so that their careers are protected. Law, religion or merely big business, all offer temptations difficult for many to resist. Power perverts even the most moral among us.

No wonder a Fatty Arbuckle might be guilty of using his power to enjoy the pleasures of the many women who flocked to his side with hopes of gaining some kind of boost in their career. "What can ya do for me, baby?" Might be answered: *"I'll do anything you want...just help my career.*

Or give me a joint.

Or give me ... give me and give me ...

We all want something. And those in power can deliver. And they do. Right into their own pockets, or bedrooms.

Right or wrong, too many people with power are perverted by it.

And kids growing up in a world of beautiful people will be hurt and mangled.

Thus one wonders just how much pain was felt when somebody like Arbuckle heard the cruel cries of: *Fat boy! Who wants you?*

So, Fatty became a comic and made himself rich and enjoyed the pleasures offered by his power and fame. Fatty Arbuckle also paid the price demanded by public jealousy, and by legal power brokers who were only interested in winning, not giving justice.

Or, was he really guilty of a crime so horrible that in the last trial people simply couldn't or wouldn't believe he had done such things to an innocent young woman in her prime?

Was he really that indifference to other's feelings, needs and lives?

Perhaps, as so many people have become convinced over the years, he was a victim of the press, of the media, of people who were jealous of his fame. Or the public greedily enjoyed the juicy stories being fed them daily by reporters who only cared about their own career, by papers interested in selling ads, and broadcast by radio stations merely interested in grand profits.

Yet, even innocent, he was imperfect. And those imperfections were used against him.

For whatever reason he had grown into a man who had little true respect for women. To him they apparently were not much more than toys to pleasure his own personal desires. He's not the first nor last to use his power to take advantage of our women.

Not only Hollywood, but Washington D.C. is continually rocked by such sex scandals involving our national leaders. Real or not has nothing to do with the effect it has on all our lives. The stories feed into our continual hunger to know what can't be truly known about those famous people out there...

And so with Fatty Arbuckle the questions remain unanswered. Innocent or not, wasn't he somehow, some way, guilty of something, some crime against women?

Without question his playing around with girls while still married to Minta hammers home the theory that he didn't have much respect for womanhood, or any understanding that love and sex were something which should be considered special. He used women. How difficult was it for him to use Virginia? And when she was complaining of anguished pain he reacted like a man who had been victimized. Having once possessed Virginia, he was not interested anymore. He'd proven his power over one more human soul.

Guilty of rape, of criminal assault or not, Fatty Arbuckle was not the kind of a man for our children to admire.

After the trials, he proved his lack of sensitivity towards women by divorcing Minta, who had stood by him so closely during his time of need. His treatment of this woman alone supports the claim that he was a self-centered, egotistical and selfish man.

To believe his statement at the trials is to disbelieve every other piece of evidence which was given by so many others. And it was reported that he had told others seven completely different stories. One quote stated he admitted to having used a piece of ice on Virginia. But can you believe everything printed or reported on cable news or—heaven forbid—the Internet?

However it is highly possible that he had told the truth in court. Yet he was fighting for his life, and a man will do anything to protect himself. In fact, Fatty could have had everything to gain by telling any lie possible to get himself off the hook.

The mystery of what happened in the hotel bedroom was never solved. Like all locked room murder mysteries there was no way of knowing what actually went on.

Like many men in a position of power and fame, Fatty Arbuckle felt he could do anything he pleased and get away with it.

Whatever he might have done to Virginia, he got away with it. But the price came high, not only to him, but to town and industry called Hollywood which suffered from the investment which they had made in films still unreleased.

Possibly the best, only real lesson to come out of the Fatty Arbuckle rape case was that no town is an island, no society can set itself up against the morality of the culture around it, especially if it is the focal point of popularity and fame.

If it hadn't been Fatty Arbuckle, it would have been someone else. Arbuckle, innocent or guilty, became the public's cause to attack the sinfulness of a town that believed itself too powerful to be touched, too important and strong to be hurt.

This was the first major scandal to come out of Hollywood and rock the world. There were others. With each one the public tightened its control over the happenings in the movie capitol of the world.

In the long run the guilt or innocence of one self-centered celebrity is of little importance. The issues involved are with us today. The Simpson trial proved beyond question the total devotion that comes to those who capture the imagination of the public. It wasn't a matter of his guilt or innocence, but a simple political issue and a race card that screamed down the halls of justice to prove money buys a good defense.

Political families such as the Kennedys or Clintons or Nixons, in fact any president or member of Congress, are tragically caught up in this kind of horrid trap; fame and power have brought public attention and the media cameras focused on their every human imperfection. Fair play is a joke. Truth is fiction and fiction becomes perceived truth. Justice means very little—winning is all that counts in the end.

Guilt?

Innocence?

Justice?

Are they words with meaning or merely words to be perverted by those who pull the power strings of the world?

And the people involved are real, living human beings caught in a public trap beyond their control. The madness is that we can never know the truth, only what is fed to us through the eyes of others who have their own ax to grind, their own careers to build at the expense of all those public figures so easy to attack.

And the price they all pay can be tragic destruction of reputations, careers, fortunes, and lives. Innocent or guilty? Who cares? The public's hunger for juicy tidbits has been satisfied.

And so it continues without end. A morality play that offers no real solution.

For Hollywood it all began with Fatty Arbuckle. And it rages even today in the headlines, on the cable news and most of all dominates the Internet and our every day lives!

PART TWO

THE WILLIAM DESMOND TAYLOR MURDER CASE

The William Desmond Taylor murder mystery was, in many ways, a convoluted event, which, in the end, had a major effect on the history of the town's early development. It became one of the turning points that set public outrage down a roller coaster ride to censorship.

In those early years of Hollywood, at the beginning of the 1900s, silent films communicated images of life in the United States. Every film depicted its own concept of the American dream—or exposed its nasty under-belly that few wished for the world to see.

The city sucked young talent right through, into the gates of all the major studios and out the back door, never to be heard from again. But a few lucky ones did become major filmmakers in the coming decades. They all clamored for fame and fortune in this newly developing industry: artists, actors, writers, cameramen, musicians, producers and directors. And they would combine their special talents to influence not only the American scene but also the whole world.

In the early years the technical film effects were limited, and the flickering images on the screen somewhat grainy by twenty-first century standards. But even then, they had developed some very slick tricks. Today, we find many of these landmark films offered VHS, DVD, cable and endless various media sources. Awkward by today's standards, they still stand up artistically. And their influence on American culture, and across the world, continues to be dynamic.

The fact that these screen images were nothing but illusion, fantasy make-believe didn't matter. Reality had little to do with filmmaking. Illusion and special effects ruled the day from the very beginning—just as it does now with such magic demonstrated in the Star Wars epics and other fantasy films that brazenly dazzle modern movie goers today.

But there was a major problem.

The depiction of our cultural morals became a concern to the leaders of all the major studios.

Interestingly enough, these early years were amazingly tame by our standards today where just about anything goes in full stereo surround sound and vivid living color on huge screens (or even in the privacy of our Home Theaters via DVD players). But it was a long, twisting pathway to get to where we stand today. Back then, during the early part of the twentieth century, the film industry was a new and virgin territory, being fashioned out of the minds, skills, imaginations and technology of the times. Masterpieces such as D. W. Griffith's *Birth of a Nation* would rock the country on many levels, both socially and technically. This was an experimental period that seemed to offer unlimited horizons for exploration. It was the socially acceptable limits which were being explored and defined that shocked the public and concerned the filmmakers as a result. In the end, the Hays Office took on the responsibility of censoring what was permitted on the screens of American movie theaters. Without their approval a film would not get distributed. They controlled the content of what was offered to the public at large. During its control, Hollywood was presenting lovely, ideally painted cultural fantasy. The product it offered up was nothing like it is today. The modern rating system has opened the creative doors that had been crushed shut.

Getting from there to here was a troubled period.

* * * * * * *

In the beginning, there were few official controls. It was the massive public cries of moral outrage that forced the forming of the Hays Office. Now the rules would be dramatically changed. Hollywood must be squeaky clean! And it was white washed! Behind the scenes, of course, little changed. It was all illusion.

Truth was not the issue.

Dreamland and most of all, the images of the world of "sin & vice" had made fortunes for smart promoters. These men ruled the early days of Hollywood.

But not all of the powerful filmmakers were lacking strong moral values—these men and women would soon rule the day! In fact they would soon ram their stamp of right & wrong onto every frame of film released. In the name of God and protection of children, the Hays Office soon controlled Hollywood's censorship scissors. Kisses, which had been vampish and racy in the '20s, became quick pressing of lips! Heaven forbid they should last too long!

But here we are concerned with the early years, before censorship, which served as the dynamite to power later reform.

What was put on film had little to do with the reality behind the scenes. The Casting Couch was a norm, and starlets were all too often little more than sex toys generously shared by anyone willing to play with them. Morality on film was one thing, on the couch it was "take what you can get"—just keep it "hush-hush!" The history of the film industry is cluttered with juicy scandals, from the beginning years and right into the twenty-first century.

All anyone had to do was to imagine their favorite film star coming into their arms in a passionate embrace before the camera. The idea of continuing the scene in private would be a natural temptation.

And the bait was always there, and would always be blatantly offered up on a platter to those who wanted to enjoy the tasty treats spread out so generously before them.

The transformation of Hollywood from a city of sin to an uptight town of moral prudery was to take its own sweet time.

It was, in the end, the power of the press (and radio) which forged change. Once the stories reached the public, there was no controlling the resulting outcome. Just like today.

Who doesn't love a mystery?

And who isn't fascinated by murder in a locked room?

And if these events involve celebrities, all the more intriguing and exciting.

The William Desmond Taylor case was an ideal puzzle that captured the attention of the public and the law. It was destined to fascinate the minds of all those who followed the story, a true combination of murder and fame. And it involved some of Hollywood's most famous stars.

It was during the Fatty Arbuckle trials that the director, William Desmond Taylor, was found dead. The effects of this murder were felt not only by those directly involved with the Taylor case but they also influenced the Arbuckle juries and contributed to the final ruin of the comic's career.

Hollywood had been releasing motion pictures that were said to "burn up the screen." (Today those old films seem corny and possibly only mildly warm, considering the products of later years. Many of them can be seen on Turner Classic Movies, a free gift to the serious movie fan.)

How things have changed.

Today's visual and verbal expression—from sexual to moral—would have been considered shocking. Even GP movies would have shocked. R ratings totally outrageous. X, beyond consideration other than as "never spoken of" stag films, seen only in private, secretly obtain from highly questionable and shady distributors.

But back then Hollywood itself was a totally different place. Not like today, which is, in reality, a mere illusion backed by the huge HOLLYWOOD sign that still hangs over the town in the hills above the city.

In the beginning Hollywood was a private little settlement, a closed-circuit society, much tighter than even a small town community, where everyone knows what everyone else is doing. There was the famous "grapevine," a communication system as fast as any modern scientific means of communication. Almost as quick as today's Internet.

And, of course, there were the movie fan magazines, which cluttered the newsstands of America with their fantasy stories about the Hollywood stars.

This was the Hollywood which lived through prohibition as a wide open, wild town that sported free flowing illegal liquor, gave expensive "blow-outs" that were then among the national topics of conversation. What went on in Hollywood was the envy of everyone in the country. Movie people lived in style. And that not only included guzzling of bootleg booze, but also the patronizing of the Chinatown heroin dens. Hollywood was the center of glamour and also was the cesspool of every type of immorality. The New Babylon.

While the events of the Arbuckle case were shocking the public, the scandalous implications of the Taylor murder stunned everyone so much that it became necessary to take desperate measures to bring an end to the bad publicity which was beginning to center on the movie capitol.

The case was never solved.

William Desmond Taylor was chief director of the Famous Players-Lasky studios. He was one of the most handsome executives Hollywood had to offer. His private life was highly active, including some of the most important actresses in town, especially Mabel Normand and Mary Miles Minter who became directly involved in the investigations surrounding his death. Either one maybe could have been responsible for his murder.

William Taylor's body was found on February 2, 1922, at eight o'clock in the morning, by his butler Henry Peavey, in the study of his expensive bungalow at Westlake, Los Angeles.

At first, Peavey had no suspicion that his employer had been murdered. He believed that the death had been caused by a heart attack.

The police had other ideas.

As the investigation continued, several theories developed.

One of two famous ladies of the motion pictures may have killed him in a fit of jealousy.

There were other theories.

Edward Sands, a former butler who had run out after robbing his employer, killed Taylor in the attempt to avoid prosecution.

A member of the Los Angeles narcotics ring found it necessary to put an end to Taylor's investigations and his private efforts to expose narcotic leaders.

An unknown person, trying to steal the love letters written to him by Mabel Normand—possibly to be used for blackmailing purposes—shot and killed him.

The "grapevine" crackled with the news almost before the reporters had been alerted. Today's Internet couldn't have been faster in alerting the community. So it didn't matter "when" the newspaper announced that Mr. Taylor had been murdered. It was late in informing the Hollywood colony. Those personally involved with Taylor were quickly forewarned. They had already prepared themselves for the police investigations that followed.

One of the first theories, which might have explained the killing, was quickly eliminated. The position of Taylor's body on the study floor initially suggested the possibility that he had been the victim of an attempted robbery. One fact decidedly proved that this wasn't the case. His wallet with $120 in cash was untouched. His gold signet ring hadn't been removed from his finger. The fact that the bullet wound and the hole in his waistcoat didn't line up, suggested that Taylor wasn't in a normal relaxed position when he was shot and killed. This caused the belief that his arms had been held high over his head. But it was soon pointed out that this wasn't the only possibility. Taylor might have been embracing a woman. Investigations proceeded along that line of reasoning. The discovery of a pink nightgown that was still surrounded with the aroma of seductive perfume in Taylor's wardrobe gave fire to the idea that the assassin might have been a woman.

Mabel Normand suddenly appeared, saying that Taylor had letters, which she wished to claim in order to keep their contents from the newspapers. The letters, the police reported, were never found.

In the months that followed, Miss Normand insisted that nothing intimate had ever developed between herself and Taylor, and that they'd only been good friends. The African-American butler-valet, Peavey, claimed otherwise. He stated that the actress had once said that she and Taylor were planning to get married.

The search for letters did not reveal any that Miss Normand had claimed. But it did turn up very passionate and suggestive ones by Mary Miles Minter; another famous feminine star who had a screen and public image of being the pure, innocent young woman, who would never *think* of becoming intimately involved with a man without a morally and spiritually blessed marriage.

So much for Hollywood images.

From the very beginning, the Taylor murder was a baffling mystery that shook and shocked Hollywood to its very foundations. One thing the Hollywood crowd didn't know about, was the secret which the man, who called himself William Desmond Taylor, had kept from all his personal and professional associates. It was the police who discovered the truth about Taylor's real identity.

Taylor had been born William Cunningham Deane Tanner in 1877, and was the oldest son of an upper-class Irish family which resided in Mallow, County Cork. William Tanner was expected to have had a military career. His grandfather had been a Conservative M.P. and his father was a British army colonel. He was, in fact, groomed and raised on the belief that he'd be joining the Royal Engineers (via Sandhurst). Up until the time he graduated from Clifton College, William Tanner's plans had been for an army career. Either just before graduation or shortly afterwards the young man became interested in acting and after leaving college he joined the Manchester theatrical company. Here he learned the ground rules of acting. Then he suddenly appeared in Canada as an engineer. During the Klondike gold rush, William Tanner followed the thousands who were seeking their fortunes. There seems to be no record as to what kind of strike young Tanner made, if any, but the time he spent in the Klondike must have made some dramatic personal changes in his life. He was living with the most rugged of men, fighting both the cold elements and the Klondike topography in an attempt to strike it rich.

In his early twenties, at the turn of the century, Tanner appeared in New York. He was now an outstandingly handsome young man. His good looks, emphasized by a neatly trimmed British-type moustache and accent, made him a popular figure with the women. His effect on those who were introduced to him was sharp enough and impressive enough to gain opportunities to follow many careers. His knowledge of cultural things, and especially of art and antiques, for which he had a sound and realistic business knowledge, gained him the position of junior partner for one of the most exclusive firms in the city. William Tanner became highly popular and successful. This more than pleased his senior partners and business associates. He was personable, handsome, cultured and well versed in the antique business. He was the type of man for whom a future success in the business world was assured. William Tanner was going to become one of the most successful of New York tycoons.

His future was completely secured when he met Ethel Harrison. Miss Harrison was a member of the famous musical comedy team called the "Floradora." The New York social world, in which he circulated, quickly became accustomed to seeing the young couple together and it was no surprise when they finally married.

There seemed to be no reason to believe that the young newly-weds weren't very happy. Their future place in society was fixed. Tanner's professional position was gaining quite a reputation. They had a daughter and the future looked very promising indeed.

Tanner had a younger brother who had served as a British officer during the Boer War in Africa. In 1906 he suddenly appeared in New York where he managed to impress the city's art world enough to obtain a managerial position at one of the art companies. In a short time he married, and now the two brothers were finally settled and were circulating in the same social set.

But something was missing for William Tanner. Maybe it was excitement. Possibly being so well off both socially and professionally made him feel a lack of challenge. Maybe it was the responsibility of having a family. Regardless of position and future, regardless of the high salary and attractive wife and daughter, Tanner began to feel restless, began to think of his situation as a trap. It could easily be that he discovered he wasn't cut out for married life, or the New York business world.

The outward signs of his uneasiness revealed themselves in his heavy drinking habits, but nobody guessed this indicated any real unhappiness or marital problems.

Then suddenly and unexpectedly the man known as William Tanner disappeared.

This happened some years after his brother's arrival in New York, in October 1912. His last morning at home was a pleasant and affectionate one. He kissed his wife and daughter and then left the home, which he now apparently thought of as a personal trap. After going to his bank and withdrawing a large sum of money he silently faded out of existence. According to all records and reports it was at the bank that William Cunningham Deane Tanner was last seen.

One can only imagine the pain and sorrow which his wife and daughter must have felt at the loss of husband and father. Days and weeks of agony followed. Weeks faded into months and months into years, until all hopes were gone.

Theories as to his disappearance simply offered no satisfactory answer to his whereabouts.

There was no doubt that William Tanner had taken a large amount of money from the bank. If it had been for a business deal, or as a stake for a new life, his wife would not know until many years later. It was possible that Tanner had some deal in the offing, and after having taken the money from the bank had been robbed, beaten, killed and his body somehow hidden. At the end of two years without any word as to the fate of her husband, Mrs. Tanner, now apparently believing he had walked out on her, got a legal divorce to clear herself from any ties with the man who had been her husband for so many years. In a short time she married the owner of the famous Delmonico's Restaurant, a marriage which was fruitful and rewarding.

Following his brother's example, Dennis Tanner did the same kind of disappearing act, and was never officially heard from again. Perhaps William had in some way contacted Dennis, although there is no real evidence of this. Some years later, when William had added Desmond Taylor to his name, there was reason to believe that his brother turned up as a butler, under the name of Edward Sands.

Any record of William Tanner, either under his own name or an assumed name, was never found until the year 1915. It is known and recorded on the official record of the Flying Corps of the Canadian Army that a man by the name of William Desmond Taylor enlisted for service in 1915. He had become Captain within the span of two years in the service of the Flying Corps. There is no question of William's ability. He was well educated and could do almost anything if he put his mind to it. In later years he kept the title of Captain because he felt it added to his stature. He had never served in any active action during his stay in the service.

Though it is easy to be harsh with the kind of man who would walk out on his wife and daughter, it is also fair to consider the fact that he apparently was the type of person who was searching for something that would give him personal satisfaction; a place which would make him happy and contented.

We all search for some escape from the harsh real world, which can, at times, seem highly restrictive. We all long for something "better" which is almost always illusive. It is this hunger that drives the dream-machine in Hollywood that creates the illusionary world, which can only exist on film. We all wish for something better. It was this inner hunger that drove people like Norma Jean Baker to become Marilyn Monroe, just to name one of countless actors who beg for fame on the streets of Hollywood. Each and every one was driven by a very strong obsession that made them famous.

Taylor was nonetheless a selfish and self-centered man who was fully aware of his attractiveness to the opposite sex and his abilities as a person to do far greater things than he'd done in the past. And, apparently, didn't care who was hurt in the process of getting his way. Maybe a driving sense of uneasiness, a lack of true direction and challenge moved him and drove him to his destiny.

There are many people like this. There are many men who cannot face the responsibilities of fatherhood and marriage, who run from life trying to find some sanctuary that will feed their egos. Such people like these, who reveal a great front and show of conceit, are really very insecure. Also, a person who finds things too easy will find life itself a struggle, because they will get no personal satisfaction out of their accomplishments.

Others, like Taylor, do, in time, find a place where they can enjoy some measure of contentment. When they finally mature enough to compromise with themselves and life, they realize that their ideals are impractical and that reality and life are heavy with unhappiness, with defeats, with imperfection.

With William Tanner the role of William Desmond Taylor offered the very thing he had so craved as a younger man: entrance into the dramatic world of acting. Nobody can ever really probe the Tanner half of Taylor's personality because it had been secret for too many years.

Taylor used women, but apparently didn't do so against their will. It had been the "Taylor" part of him that had taken over when he'd walked out on his wife—and which created, for the world, a series of pictures that gave enjoyment and pleasure to all who saw them.

Is that justification enough to forgive his sins? Probably not. But to the man, it apparently was what made life worth living.

After the First World War, Captain William Desmond Taylor suddenly appeared on the Hollywood scene. He was without money, without position. The only thing he had was the same ability and same personal attractiveness and charm, which had always been with him. He was no more naked in Hollywood as William Taylor was when he'd been in New York as William Tanner.

It just happened that the town had the elements he most needed to succeed.

Hollywood was ripe for a man of Taylor's ability. He was not only good looking but very well educated. His breeding was flavored with just the right amount of intriguing bad manners, which only the elite had perfected to a magnificent and attractive art. His early training as an actor and the experience he'd acquired in New York at the executive level of business now combined to make him a prime catch for the Hollywood movie colony.

What a wonderful place to develop a new identity to its fullest—and create a life ideally suited to this new illusion of reality.

Anybody who might remember an actor by the name of William Desmond will be able to picture the handsome man. He had shaved his moustache in order to be acceptable for the screen image of a leading male actor. Moustaches were, at this time, saved as devices for villains. He'd started as a bit actor. His ability was quickly noticed. From there on it was an easy job for him to move upwards into leading roles. The studio powers learned that their man, William Desmond, was not only a talented actor but also had the ability to direct and produce. They moved him into the executive branch of the movie making business. This kind of swift promotion probably couldn't have happened later—he had arrived at the right time to use his multiple talents to their best effect.

By 1920 Taylor was making as much as $40,000 a year for his services. For the times the salary was impressive, but no more so than his films. Today it might seem that the pictures which Taylor was responsible for are rather ridiculous, but for their times they were highly popular with the public. They were even acclaimed as powerful and extremely professional.

The 1920s were a different world from that which we live in today. Prohibition was going into full swing. Young people were living, what their elders considered, wild lives. Those, who would never have consumed liquor, became heavy drinkers. It was the thing to do. The Marx Brothers were making a hit on Broadway. Jazz was beginning to show signs of national popularity, though the Benny Goodmans, Tommy Dorseys, Ellingtons, Basies were yet to come. This was an age of social and moral revolution. The ideas and moralities of the American culture were being turned upside down. Before the 20's women, who went to bars, were labeled tramps—but the speakeasies were the now only real "in" places to be seen. Where this generation's mothers had never admitted to enjoying sex, it suddenly became the vogue for young girls to admit the fact that they had liked the sexual, even in marriage. The whole nation was breaking the law and becoming boozers—and drinks loosened the resistance of the young ladies to the point where they could almost claim respectability and still have wildly swinging nights with their lovers. The social barriers were still officially up, and the nation refused to publicly admit that these changes were for the best. The twenties were roaring in every way. Half the population was shaking their heads in shock and moral disgust at the other half enjoying a wild time.

And for this new public scene, William Desmond Taylor was directing films which delighted millions. He joined the Famous Players-Lasky Corporation as a director.

Hollywood, itself, at this time, was almost broken up into two little communities—those elite who lived in mansions, and those who lived in the "village" type courts made up of attractive bungalows. Everything was beautifully landscaped in such "courts" which were built with the idea of raw elegance. They were show places for the public that was never allowed more than the right to look from afar, or see in film fan magazines. While such living might seem strangely confining for people with money, it actually served two purposes: it helped keep alive the close-knit village air about Hollywood and it also worked to the advantage of those living in the "courts." Any party given by one of the tenants became a "community" affair. The fact that everybody around was working in the movie industry made each party an automatic success. Although everybody was well aware of your private life, this didn't seem to bother people very much. What your neighbors might know about you, you knew about them. It went both ways, thus became a self-serving mutual agreement to keep the "silence"!

Taylor, as has been noted, lived at Westlake and his bungalow was well known in the Hollywood community. He'd decorated it quite differently from the rest of the movie crowd. His knowledge of art, furniture and decoration gave him a reputation as a man of refined taste.

During this time it was considered impressive to have a large supply of vases and impressive tiger rugs. Such things were considered elegant and a show of wealth, and glamour. It was important to keep up a plush and showy front. But Taylor didn't bend completely to this requirement. He did, however, have a number of vases and sported the necessary tiger rugs. He also had a large and impressive collection of books. His study had the appearance of a space for work rather than a show place to impress guests. His favorite dark stained colonial furniture helped to create a relaxed and cool atmosphere. His collection of books included volumes of science, aviation and psychology. While other members of the Hollywood set enjoyed impressing guests with their large oil paintings, he favored simple wood-cuts. William Taylor enjoyed the classic and the attractive, without being unduly showy. He felt that taste was more important that mere flash. He impressed others, not by his lack of show but by his extremely fine judgment and cultured awareness of what was truly art.

Hollywood, more than any place else, has a seedy reputation of attracting men who take advantage of their positions to obtain the favors of the "ladies in waiting." There were many such women who were willing to do anything necessary to get parts in films. With somebody like William Desmond Taylor, one of the more popularly known directors for the Famous Players-Lasky Studios, it was not just the struggling young starlets, but the "Queens" themselves who vied for his attention. He was handsome enough to attract such ladies merely on his irresistible physical appearance alone. The motives many of the women had for dating him may have been mainly to build their careers, but certainly a natural sexual attraction for the man was a desirable bonus. There is no doubt that the most attractive and popular actresses of the time who were competing for his attentions had no need to play the casting couch game. Some of them were already in a position to pick and choose directors. And it is even possible that he was wooing them to star in latest film. If Taylor managed, like many in his position, to use less known actresses merely as sex toys, no one really knew. One can guess that he played a selfish and cruel game of offering empty promises for a quick tumble on the couch with many lovely, unsophisticated struggling actresses.

But two women who were nationally known actresses were reported to have gone into a rage against one another, in a "cat" fight over the affections of this handsome director.

With fame and power in the film industry came public recognition of a different kind.

64

Anybody who had appeared in pictures as Taylor did in the beginning of his Hollywood career, especially after having walked out on a wife and daughter, must have realized that, in time, he would be recognized.

It was in the latter part of 1920s that Ethel, his former wife, and their eighteen-year-old daughter Daisy happened to see a picture which starred "William Desmond." It must have been a shock for Ethel to suddenly see her lost husband on the screen. Though, luckily, she had been remarried too long to feel any real shattering pain at discovering that William Tanner was still alive.

Strangely enough, events that followed this discovery were surprisingly without any apparent hostilities.

When Taylor received a letter from his daughter and former wife, which was actually quite friendly and surprisingly understanding, he was delighted and quickly answered it expressing his happiness to have heard from Ethel after so many years. After a correspondence had developed, Taylor made arrangements to meet his daughter in New York.

The meeting was warm and affectionate and developed an immediate closeness between father and daughter.

Was it fatherly love or guilt that motivated this new relationship with a woman he hardly knew? Who knows?

Interestingly enough, he felt no real emotional attachments for the many ladies who shared his bed. Perhaps they were mutually agreeable affairs, payments of sexual favors for parts in films. Yet many women—some famous—actually fell under his spell. He had little interest in a seriously binding relationship. That marriage was out of the question is revealed by that fact that Taylor left all his money to his daughter, a gesture which was merely symbolic, since she was the step-daughter of one of New York's millionaires.

A short time later there were rumors in Hollywood that Captain Taylor was romantically involved with Mabel Normand and that marriage was only a matter of time. It was even believed, by some, that the couple was secretly engaged, though neither actually admitted to this, publicly.

Mabel Normand was famous for her roles in the Mack Sennett slapstick comedies and, in time, had become one of Charlie Chaplin's leading ladies.

The match seemed unnatural, considering that Taylor was mainly a snobbish intellectual, a heavy reader and highly cultured, while Mabel Normand was the complete opposite, both in her attitude about life and her reading habits. Though she was a highly talented female comic and quite a catch, even for Taylor, Mabel wasn't his intellectual match, and was known for being difficult to get along with. There is a high possibility that he was attracted to this "opposite" and considered Mabel all the more attractive for her so-called disabilities. Whether he was actually in love is debatable. Neither of them denied the engagement rumors, which circulated. Possibly they were either thinking about it, or perhaps believed it didn't do any harm to let the Hollywood gossips have their fun. Possibly it made Mabel Normand feel more "respectable" if others believed that their relationship wasn't on a casual level—or maybe she actually believed that in time they would be getting married.

It was all rather contrary to Taylor's apparent contempt for the women who came into his life.

In December of 1920 a dim suggestion that there was more to the Taylor-Normand romance than met the eye entered the picture. Taylor had his chauffeur, Earl Tiffany, drive him to Los Angeles' Chinatown for the purpose of finding one of the many secret "heroin" parties for which this little settlement was known. Chinatown was one of the favorite hangouts for many of the Hollywood crowd because of this easy heroin connection. One of the more sordid realities of being famous and having lots of money is discovering that this doesn't always buy happiness. Far too many people patronized the Chinatown heroin dens in a search for escape from that harsh truth.

William Desmond Taylor, for all his self-centered, selfish life style was, quite obviously, a complex a person, not just one-sided. That he was a user of women is obvious, that he could actually develop real feelings is indicated by his quick connection with a daughter he hadn't known for years. And of course he was a complex man—multi-sided, intelligent, cultured and talented. He couldn't have created so many successful films without having sensitivity to the world at large. Naturally, there were people he actually cared about, whose lives could touch him in a serious manner.

And it was this side of the man that motivated him down an interesting pathway, not without its personal dangers: China-town's heron dens.

Taylor wasn't a user. What he wanted was to find the pushers, the men responsible for supplying heroin for addicts. His motive, it turned out, was the desire to bring justice to those who were responsible for hooking a very close female friend. Friends warned him that this was a dangerous game that could end his career. Taylor's determination suggested that his friend was Mabel Normand.

It didn't take Taylor long to get some of the information he'd been looking for. When he walked into the United States Attorney's office to see Assistant Attorney Green, he felt that he had enough evidence to warrant the help of the police. He not only knew those responsible for the actual peddling, but he could also name the boss of the Los Angeles heroin ring. He wanted assistance to get more evidence. Green assigned two officers to help Taylor, even though the man felt the investiga-tion was doomed to failure. Getting names was one thing, but to find the proof which could be used in a court of law was another matter. All the witnesses who could have helped to close the heroin dens simply refused to admit anything in public.

Green later said that he felt the investigation, which Taylor had instigated, had made him a prime target for the nar-cotic bosses who couldn't afford exposure. Any attempts at dis-closure had to be stopped. Those who were responsible for the investigation would have to pay the price.

These actions of Taylor, at this time, surely led to the suspicion that a member of this heroin ring might have assassi-nated him. Possibly, he had actually obtained the final evidence that he needed in order to put the pushers in jail and he was, for this reason, killed.

There is another event that served as possible motive for Taylor's murder. It took place sometime before his death.

He had a man, by the name of Edward Sands, as a secre-tary-valet, who became very popular with Taylor's guests.

Sands was a personable man who spoke with an English accent. Though Sands and Taylor were employee and employer in public, there's some evidence that they were very close in private. When Taylor went to Europe in 1921, there is reason to believe that the man who stole a majority of his suits, grabbed all available cash and forged Taylor's name on a number of checks, was Edward Sands, who had disappeared by the time his employer had returned. If, as was later believed possible, Edward Sands was merely an assumed name for Dennis Tanner, Taylor's brother, it would explain the director's lack of interest in accusing the missing secretary-valet or making any attempt to find the man. On the other hand, if Sands hadn't been Taylor's brother, it seems reasonable to consider him responsible for killing Taylor in an attempt to stop any prosecution that might be taken because of the robbery.

It was on the First of February in 1922, sometime during the evening, that William Desmond Taylor was shot.

According to those who are known to have seen Taylor during this night, the evening seemed to be quite peaceful and ordinary. There was no indication of what was so soon to follow. Peavey, the colored valet, told the police that he'd given Taylor a simple dinner at 6:30 p.m. and at seven a car arrived with Mabel Normand.

According to Peavey, she had her chauffeur wait while she went in and had cocktails with Taylor. Peavey heard the two talking in subdued voices for about forty-five minutes, then Taylor left the house with Miss Normand, taking the girl to her car. After cleaning the glasses Peavey waited until his employer returned to the house, at which time, around 8:00, he left, having finished the day's work.

It was about an hour later that William Desmond Taylor was shot and killed. Neighbors were never quite sure of the time, since they either didn't hear the gunshot or assumed it to be a car backfiring in the street. Around three hours later, Edna Purviance, famous as another of Charlie Chaplin's leading ladies, saw that the light was still on in Taylor's study.

The next morning Peavey stepped into the bungalow to start his morning's work. He went into the study to clean up and discovered Taylor lying face up stretched out on the floor. A chair had fallen over his legs and his hands were resting neatly at his side, almost touching the seams of his trousers.

The colored butler quickly called the police and within minutes an ambulance had arrived. On quick examination it was revealed that the man hadn't had a heart attack, as the servant believed. He had been shot in the back, on his left side. The bullet had come to a stop in his neck. The wound must have caused instantaneous death. It was quickly established that he had lain there for at least ten hours. The murderer had taken the time to arrange Taylor's body in the "pose" in which it was found, and must have felt for some personal reason that leaving the chair across the man's legs was a final touch of ironic poetry.

Taylor had been in the process of filling out his income tax report, which was left half-finished when his unknown killer arrived.

The bullet that killed him came from a .38 revolver. As has been pointed out before, the hole it made in his body didn't match the one that was in his waistcoat, giving reason for the theory that he had either been killed while embracing a woman or while holding his arms high above his head.

The fact that neither his gold signet ring nor the $120 in his wallet had been touched, eliminated the robbery motive.

The idea of a woman assassin became the prime theory, which the police worked on, even though there was evidence to negate the idea of Taylor having been killed while holding a woman in his arms. The original theory that some woman had embraced him and then pulled the trigger of a gun hidden in her hands seemed incredible. When no evidence of powder burns was discovered, this theory had to be discarded.

The speed at which the news of Taylor's death traveled through the Hollywood community is revealed by the fact that Mabel Normand showed up, while the police were still there. She claimed that she wanted to retrieve letters that she'd sent Taylor over the months, that might, if the papers got hold of them, be embarrassing.

The police did search the house and found not only letters, but also a lady's nightgown. The letters weren't Mabel Normand's but from another young actress, Mary Miles Minter.

Next to Mary Pickford, Miss Minter was the darling of the films, famous for her roles as a "sweet sixteen" love struck girl, who wouldn't think of ever becoming involved with anything scandalous. Of course not! The roles of innocent country girls doing battle against the evil villains had not only become a professional image, but fans innocently believed it to be the real Mary Miles Minter. She was, according to those who knew her in Hollywood, far from the sweet young thing, but actually snobbish, pompous and superior acting towards those around her. She was quoted as saying to a reporter, *"I do not care for any praise but that of my mother."* Mrs. Charlotte Shelby, her mother, was the only one who actually had any control over her twenty-year-old daughter, and had managed to stop all serious romances in which Mary got involved.

Mary Minter was the last person anybody would have thought to get involved with the famous director. Top that off with the fact that "everybody" *knew* about his supposed engagement with Mabel Normand and Hollywood had a first rate conversation piece even more exciting than the puzzle concerning Taylor's killer.

The letters were embarrassingly cluttered with words of love and affection, written in a stiff childish scrawl—many of which were printed in a code that the police quickly broke. Lines like the following, printed in the national papers, drew the shocked attention of Miss Minter's fans:

What shall I call you, you wonderful man?

I want to go away with you to the hills or anywhere, just so that we can be alone all close in a beautiful little woodland cottage...I would sweep and dust—they make the sweetest little dust cups, you know—and tie fresh ribbons on snowy white curtains and feed birds, fix flowers...and in my spare time I would darn your socks...I would go to my room and put on something soft and flowing, then I would lie on the couch and wait for you...then I would...find two strong arms around me, two dear lips pressed against mine in a long sweet kiss.

All her letters were signed much like this one. *"Dearest, I love you—I love you—I love you,"* with a series of x's to indicate all the kisses she was bestowing on her lover.

The surprise of discovering that Captain Taylor was privately seeing another woman while openly dating Miss Normand caused a flutter of shock through the Industry, and especially to any of the Hollywood stars who had been connected romantically with Taylor.

Mabel Normand claimed that the friendship between herself and Taylor was nothing more than that of a young woman seeking the companionship of a "father."

Mary Miles Minter also refused to admit anything more than friendship with Taylor, claiming that the words were merely those of deep affection and that she would never have done anything to hurt Mabel Normand whom "I loved...and I want the whole world to know it." But later Miss Minter was forced to change her story to some extent; because of the publication of the more intimately revealing letters.

As to Mabel Normand, her denial that anything intimate was going on between her and Taylor was contradicted by Peavey's statement to the police. He recalled that,

> One night, when Miss Normand was invited to Captain Taylor's home for dinner she called me and said that she and Captain Taylor were going to get married...then she asked me what other girls dined with Captain Taylor. I told her that there was only one—Miss Normand...she laughed and said that the Captain had me well trained.

When confronted with this information and asked if she had ever been in love with Taylor, Mabel Normand flatly denied it. When further questioned about if there was any man that might be jealous enough to kill Taylor, because of her friendship, she assured them there wasn't. When she was asked about

Peavey's statement, Miss Normand claimed that everything he said was a lie and that he should be ashamed of himself because, *"I saved his job once when Captain Taylor wanted to fire him."*

Her collapse at Taylor's funeral, with an audience of over 6,000 people, made a liar out of her. There was no doubt now that the emotional feelings towards the man had been far deeper than she'd attempted to make people believe. That evening, it was necessary to put her under the care of a doctor because of her hysterical condition.

The police not only turned Hollywood upside down in their attempt to find the Taylor killer, but also searched the nation for Edward Sands, the butler who had disappeared not too long before.

The list of possible suspects included: Mabel Normand, Mary Miles Minter, Edward Sands, an unknown member of the Los Angeles heroin ring, or an unknown intruder who was stealing Mabel Normand's letters in the hopes of using them for blackmail.

The newspapers had a heyday with the Minter letters and the development of possible suspects, but they were working on thin air, because the police department had created a tight screen around their investigations.

Eight days of hectic public newspaper announcements were made before Thomas Woolwine, from the Los Angeles D.A.'s office appeared before reporters. He to claimed that the Hollywood motion picture industry had done everything in their power to silence any witnesses, and had made payoffs to those people who might have been able to give a lead to the real killer. He believed that the pink nightgown was an important clue, and because of this, every effort had been made to hide the real facts concerning it, in an attempt to protect the investments involved in the careers of one of the two leading female suspects. He also stated that the nightgown had disappeared and hadn't been found. It never did show up, probably because it would have labeled the killer, if one were to believe Woolwine's statements.

To counter Woolwine's public announcement, the Motion Picture Directors' Association made one of their own which claimed that Captain Taylor's murder appeared to be a perfect crime from a "criminal standpoint." They didn't deny the accusations made by the D.A.'s office, possibly on the theory that a denial would be taken with a grain of salt, and to simply ignore the claim would seem to give it less importance.

The Taylor murder was never solved.

The investigations revolving around the search for Edward Sands eliminated one possible suspect.

It was a reporter who discovered that there was not only no official record of a person by the name of Edward Sands, but that "Sands" was Dennis Tanner. When the New York police finally found Dennis Tanner, the man was able to prove that he'd not been anywhere near Hollywood on February First. Even though the reporter had found evidence to prove Edward Sands to be Taylor's brother, the police never admitted this to be true.

A statement made by Mary Miles Minter eighteen months after the police had finally given up the search for Taylor's killer, might have suggested another suspect, and it certainly reversed her former statements about her emotional feelings toward the director.

> If it had not been for mother, I might some day have married William Desmond Taylor. I was ready to marry him at any time. Mother said "No." She kept us apart as long as she could. I think she was in love with him herself!

This same subtle suggestion, that it might have been Mary Minter's mother who had killed Taylor was, again, made by another of her daughters in 1937. Mrs. Margaret Filmore, Mary's sister, while taking civil action against her mother, stated to the police: *"I have protected my mother in the Taylor murder ease."*

District Attorney Fitts asked her if she was suggesting that her mother had actually killed Taylor, but Mrs. Fillmore let him know that she didn't have to answer that: A rather vague suggestion that she knew far more than she was willing to divulge.

Fitts also stated, when revealing this information, that though there seemed reason to suspect Miss Minter's mother, there was no evidence which could make it possible to reopen the case.

Thus, with a whimper, ended a long investigation which proved fruitless:

William Desmond Taylor's murder was a perfect crime.

As with Fatty Arbuckle, there were police statements to the fact that Hollywood money had paid for silence and the truth remained a mystery. In each case there were subtle suggestions as to what had actually happened, but no hard evidence was revealed and the guilty parties are free. Yet, as in Fatty Arbuckle's case, the stars suffered. Mary Miles Minter lost great popularity as a result of the letters she'd written. Mabel Normand's career was almost ruined and would have faded out much sooner but for the help of a man by the name of Paul Bern, who later was to be the center of another major scandal.

Hollywood in the 1920s survived the William Desmond Taylor murder scandal, as it had survived many others. But such cases as this finally made it necessary to dramatically change things, and a slow cleanup of the public image of Hollywood began.

Was Taylor killed by a woman, or murdered by the leaders of the Los Angeles heroin ring? Was it a killing by an intruder looking for letters, or a planned murder? Was the motive jealousy or an attempt to silence a man who knew too much?

The police never knew, but there are those in Hollywood who probably know the truth.

William Tanner had run from New York, from a wife and child, and finally appeared in Hollywood as William Desmond Taylor. Yet, in the end, he found death waiting for him. Beyond that, the questions still remain unanswered.

Of the two leading women in Taylor's personal life, Mabel Normand died in 1930 of tuberculosis, a forgotten woman, whom Hollywood had finally been forced to turn its back on, as a result of her involvement in the Taylor mystery.

Mary Miles Minter also faded out of the Hollywood picture almost immediately after the murder.

If either of these women were guilty of murder or even indirectly responsible for the man's death, they both paid the price of a ruined career and shattered life.

And nothing was gained, other than having another terribly nasty nail hammered into the city's reputation and bringing it just one step closer to massive censorship. The Hays Office would crush creative freedom in the name of morality. Only years later would the modern rating system dramatically change things.

Today the field is wide open—and sometimes one wishes that just simple smart judgment would curb unnecessary gratuitous sex and violence. To abuse the freedom of self-expression for the purpose of simply making faster bucks at the box office is, in the end, counter-productive.

Yet, the scandals continue, each generation brings its own style and slant to what hits the media tabloids. Today we have the famous celebrities being tried on cable television, condemned right before our eyes and then released as "not guilty" by a court system which is not so much interested in justice as in winning at any price. And a media basically interested in profits. Truth, too many times, gets lost in the pitch for public attention. So even today we find ourselves locked in a vicious society which allows murder and perversions of all kinds continue to run wild.

It is the human condition which no nation, empire or industry has been able to escape, no matter what methods they may use to force controls over human behavior.

For Hollywood, the battle continues, between good & evil, between sin & purity, illusion & reality. Some people may wag their fingers in horror while others chuckle in delight. Yet in the end, little changes, other than the moral outrage challenged by the demand for creative freedom.

Censorship is an evil all to itself. And we can all be thankful that the Hays Office is a matter of history and that the film rating system is now a standard which monitors what is offered to the public. Imperfect as that might be, it is far better than the alternatives.

As a result today's films are far more graphic and the public far more educated and informed.

But the battle continues; and is destined to never be fully resolved to everybody's satisfaction.

PART THREE

THE INFANT HUSBAND IN JEAN HARLOW'S LIFE

If there is any story or illustration in real life that might unquestionably be an argument for pre-marital sex, the tragic story of Paul Bern's marriage to Jean Harlow is certainly it. Real or myth, it illustrates an argument against blindly entering into a marriage without having explored intimacy previous to the wedding night. We aren't suggesting anything here other than the fact that, according to some reports that have been documented on her experience with Paul Bern, they certainly offer serious arguments for pre-marital sex.

There are as many versions of her life and times as there are people who knew her.

Her story, like so many others, is clouded and complicated by legend, myth and dreamland fantasies. Everybody offers a different version of her life.

For some she seemed to be a wonderful symbol of the hot blonde; others noted her as nothing more than an icon of a cheap woman. Probably she was something of a satire between both types. There's good reason to believe she was fairly religious and who knows how that actually affected her living style. Some claimed she was as wild as her visual image implied. She had the bra-less look long before it was to become the norm some decades later.

Jean Harlow was, in the 1930s, the sexiest Hollywood glamour queen. She was the original *Blonde Bombshell.* They said that many men just had to look at her, or talk *about* her, to experience an automatic erection. Her reputation, as a sex symbol, was worldwide. The belief that she was the hottest thing God had put on earth was the reason Paul Bern picked her as his wife. Or so it has been reported.

Some of the Paul Bern story is questionable, even if it does illustrate a very basic reality. Any woman like Jean Harlow would certainly be an attractive object for sexual desire. That was the main PR surrounding her screen persona.

The fact does remain, regardless of any speculations, fictions, even fantasies, concerning him and Jean, that he killed himself. The motives for this will remain a mystery, for one can not know for certain, exactly what did take place.

The following offers one possibility.

It seemed unbelievable that the beautiful Jean Harlow would marry such an unlikely man as Paul Bern. He wasn't the tall, good-looking Hollywood male. He was, in fact, the last person on earth anyone would have chosen for her. Actually, he was the last man on earth who should have married any woman, let alone the American Sex Symbol of the 1930s.

The marriage was publicized as one of the most important events of the year. The young couple was obviously deeply in love. When Paul Bern committed suicide a few months later the papers announced that Jean Harlow, filled with grief and anguish, had tried to take her own life.

The mystery that followed, as a result of a note, which Paul Bern left on the dressing table in front of a picture of Jean, could have ruined her career if the true meaning had then been revealed. The missive read:

> Dearest Dear, Unfortunately this is the only way to make good the frightful wrong I have done you and to wipe out my abject humiliation. You understand that last night was only a comedy.

The story of Paul Bern's life, and the mystery which surrounded his death, is the study of the hopeless search of an anguished man to find a meaning for a life which must surely have been frustrating and painful.

First, let's look at the published facts as they appeared in the papers and magazine stories during the 1930s.

Paul Bern was born in 1889 on the third day of December, in Wannsback, Germany to a Jewish couple by the name of Henrietta Hirsch and Julius Levy. He was one of eighteen children. When he was nine, his family pulled up roots, as many of their countrymen had, and immigrated to the United States. They settled in the Lower East Side of New York. When he completed high school, he became interested in acting and was reported to have won a scholarship to the Academy of Dramatic Arts. Paul centered all his energies on learning the theater. He changed his name from Levy to Bern. His efforts as an actor were unsuccessful. He was neither talented, nor attractive enough.

While he was at the Academy of Dramatic Arts, during the year 1911, Bern met Dorothy Millette. He was about to graduate when Dorothy entered the Academy at Carnegie Hall. Dorothy wanted to become a famous actress, but her dreams were never to materialize. The young couple became serious enough to consider marriage. They moved into the New York Hotel Algonquin as "man and wife," and friends believed that they were married.

Paul's failure to make any real mark for himself as an actor caused him to try directing. Between 1911 and 1914, Paul was working as both stage manager and assistant director. He managed to also act in the plays. These years provided his basic experience in show business.

When Bern appeared in *Too Many Cooks,* Dorothy was also hired to play a role in it. After that, Dorothy faded out of theater life, though she continued to live with Bern as his "wife."

They suffered long periods of financial difficulties while each of them struggled for recognition in the theater.

In 1914 Paul went to work for a Canadian motion picture company. From then on he moved from one movie company to another, until 1918 when he attracted the attention of the Goldwyn studios.

Three years later, after ten years of living together, Paul and Dorothy finally found it necessary to separate, and they parted company. Bern went on to Hollywood to become a Hollywood legend.

Dorothy, after losing Paul Bern, went into a deep depression that finally had an emotional effect over her personality. She refused to seek help from doctors. She continued living at the Algonquin until Paul's marriage to Jean Harlow.

In Hollywood, Paul worked as a film cutter and finally became an assistant director and scenarist. In time he was given the job of producing such pictures as *Open All Night* and *The Dressmaker of the Night*. These assignments gave him his reputation as a professional and as a talented producer. He impressed Hollywood with his skill as a producer and his ability for getting some of the top names to work in his pictures. People who worked for him liked Paul, finding him a very considerate and sensitive man who did everything he could for his friends. Everyone, including those who worked for him and those for whom he worked liked him. He was the type of executive who was able to stand between the talented, temperamental artist and the cold, impersonal financial backers who merely looked at their bank books and wanted to know why a picture was costing so much and bringing in so little. When the heads of Metro Goldwyn-Mayer became aware of his talents, they were anxious to sign him up to their studio.

Paul Bern was hired at $35,000 a year at Metro for which he was supposed to direct four pictures yearly. It became evident that he was even more than just an excellent director and producer. He also had a sharp sense of what was commercial, the ability to get the best out of everybody. Paul was rapidly moved up to Production supervisor and when he proved himself even better than the studio bosses might have imagined, he was placed directly under Irving Thalberg as a member of this remarkable young man's M-G-M staff.

His popularity on the M-G-M lot became so great, because of his humanitarian way of assisting those needing personal or professional help, that he was finally called "Hollywood's Father Confessor," a title, which followed him to the grave.

He was the kind of man who would do anything for a friend. No sacrifice was too great, no problem too great. Once Paul even admitted he only lived for the help he could do others—a subtle hint of the inner torment which had followed him since his teen-age years.

His pocket-book was always at the disposal of anyone in need, and it didn't matter if it was an extra, starlet, director, cameraman or a star who was on the skids. No matter who might be in trouble, Paul was the first—and many times the only—person to go to their aid.

Barbara La Marr was one who was helped by Bern when others had turned their backs on the poverty-stricken woman. Bern, at one time, was to have married Barbara, but she'd refused on the grounds that she knew he would not make a satisfactory husband. When Barbara was sick and dying, it was Paul Bern who bought her a home and saw to it that some of Los Angeles' most important doctors took care of her. When she finally died, he was deeply and personally hurt, feeling the terrible loss of a woman he had at one time wanted to marry, yet who had rejected him.

When Mabel Normand's career was breaking up because of her involvement with William Desmond Taylor, Bern did everything possible to help her get roles in pictures, prolonging the final end.

He helped such people as Nita Naldi, Rudolph Valentino, Ramon Navarro. John Gilbert owed much that he attained in motion pictures to Paul Bern's help and influence. Paul helped many of the biggest and smallest stars in Hollywood.

He had said that if he couldn't help others he would kill himself, and when the time came when he was unable to be of service to those around him, he would, in fact, kill himself.

He was obsessed with the idea of suicide and talked about it, in a clinical way, to many of his friends and business associates.

During the making of the *Red-Headed Woman*, a picture starring Clark Gable and the "Blonde Bombshell," Paul Bern and Jean Harlow became friends. They had met some years back, when Jean was still a struggling young actress, but this time around they were both on an equal level, Jean, the biggest sex symbol of the '30s, and Paul, one of the most powerful men at the studio.

Since Paul was in charge of the production it was a simple thing for the two to find time with each other. They became fast friends. Jean was considered the most attractive woman in the world, and certainly one of the most popular female stars to ever hit Hollywood. She was an extrovert, while Bern was an introvert; She was an actress, Paul a producer and in many ways partly the creator. Their personalities balanced each other. Jean found Paul Bern different from any other man she had met. Instead of attempting to seduce her body, he made love to her mind and soul, a thing that she wasn't used to at all.

Some people felt that she was used to running around with a very fast crowd and somewhat wild in her sexual adventuring. This image of Jean Harlow matched her PR persona. Many articles were assumed, by the masses, to be a true picture of the woman herself.

Other, more generous, stories assumed a different reality.

Jean once said: *"Paul loves me...for my mind, my spirit, my companionship, for me. He's paid me the highest compliment I've ever had. No man has ever loved me before for what's best in me."*

Paul Bern didn't think of Jean Harlow as the woman on the screen, the blonde bombshell, and the image that had become a symbol of sex for the whole American public. Yet, as it will be suggested, he may have very well married her on the belief that the sexiest woman in the world would be the woman that could succeed in making him into a "man." Of course, this is assuming facts, which are implied by events, though unable to prove one way or the other. We can hardly read anybody's mind, let alone one that is dead. He left little hard evidence concerning his reasons for killing himself; and what is left is simply a suicide note.

He romanced the soul and not the flesh, yet fully aware of the real, live woman rather than the shadow on the silver screen, which the public loved. Screen shadows are as illusive and deceptive as images flashing across our minds. All is make-believe. All illusion. And living up to those reputed "realities" has been damaging to more than one icon of the film industry. Sometimes people actually believed their publicity; others ignored it with contempt.

The reality behind the images is as illusive as phantoms. We can only guess at what really took place, in privacy, behind "locked doors," what really moved people in the real world. We can make conclusions based on very limited known facts.

Bern appealed to Jean because of his genius as a producer, because of his kindness and gentleness, because of his own romantic reaction toward her, which was so different from all the other men she had known. He was interested in her ideas, in her thoughts. He appealed to her as a mental equal, as a person and not as a sex symbol.

And how seductive this must have been to Jean, the woman.

Instead of going out to flashy restaurants, they would go on walks, talking, just enjoying each other's company. It was a story book romance. It fit into the code of morality which fiction writers were loading on the public in such lines as "death rather than dishonor." Paul Bern was the classic example of this fictional morality in a world that had just come out of the Roaring Twenties. Wild women, wild booze, wild parties. And Jean fell completely for this new, ideal, romantic courting—as any woman. Jean had had her fill of being thought of as a dumb blonde who had nothing more to offer than a quick hot roll in the hay. It has been stated that Jean Harlow, at this time, had sexual relations only with the husband she'd married at sixteen. And even though this seems somewhat difficult to believe, it does not lessen the impact of such an approach that Paul Bern offered. There is every reason to believe she was still romantic enough to honestly crave the kind of attention Paul was giving her.

Jean and Paul Bern applied for a marriage license on June 22, 1932.

Jean's private agent and personal friend, Arthur Landau claimed to have no knowledge of what was going on until Jean suddenly called him in the middle of the night, saying she wanted him to come over to her house to meet the man she was going to marry. Some people find it difficult to believe his story about Jean; but it stands as a public record as he reported it.

Jean, by this time, was the biggest thing in pictures and was making a salary of twelve hundred and fifty dollars a week at M-G-M. She had made her first picture, *The Saturday Night Kid,* in 1929. And then she rocketed to stardom in *Hell's Angels* in 1930, which was followed with *Public Enemy* with James Cagney, *The Secret Six* with Clark Gable, *The Iron Man* with Lew Ayres, *Goldie* with Spencer Tracy, *The Platinum Blonde* with Loretta Young, and *Three Wise Girls* with Mae Clarke. *The Best of the City* with Walter Huston was released in 1932, followed by *The Red-Headed Woman* with Charles Boyer.

A story-legend of Jean Harlow's discovery is told in an article by Frank Condon, which was published in *The Saturday Evening Post.* He claimed that a director in Kansas City, in front of the Kehoe's Drug Store had discovered Jean. The author wrote:

> The director sat up and said to his assistant: "Sweet spirits of Pomona, look at that hair! Go on over, Joe, and ask the girl would she like to bust into the movies, and get her 'name right'."

According to that legend she had been suddenly picked up off the streets because of her platinum blonde hair, and rocketed to immediate fame. It was only one of the many Hollywood myths. Sad to say there are many, none of which tell the total truth, and certainly at best are shaded and colored.

It was Howard Hughes who actually had been responsible for making the picture *Hell's Angels*, which made her an overnight sensation starting the Harlow legend.

This was the woman that all men desired, all men found irresistible.

And Paul Bern, a small, rather shy man, with no apparent attractiveness, had captured this "bombshell;" a mystery which everybody found hard to explain.

Arthur Landau, according to his "questionable" account, was pleased to discover that Paul Bern was to be the bridegroom. He felt that Paul would be a great help to Jean, and believed the man was all that his reputation might have promised.

While Paul had always dated many of Hollywood's leading ladies when going to movie-land parties, he had never really been connected with any scandal. It was true that he kept a mistress who lived in a West Hollywood bungalow. This arrangement was terminated upon his engagement to Jean Harlow.

From the point of the engagement, things moved fast. The Harlow legend and the mystery of Paul Bern's death are as follows.

The marriage took place in Jean's mother's home, with California Superior Judge Leon Yankwich performing the ceremony. John Gilbert was best man, and things went smoothly throughout the simple ceremony. The wedding reception was not given until the next day and all the important people of Hollywood, from Louis B. Mayer to Louella Parsons were there to extend the happy couple their congratulations. This celebration was held in the home in which Paul Bern had lived before the marriage and which he had given to Jean as a wedding present. Jean had a personal appearance to make during that afternoon. Her business activities made it impossible for the couple to go on a honeymoon.

During the next days everything seemed happy for the newlyweds. They spent as much time by themselves as possible. Days slowly blended into weeks and the only signs that there might be any friction between them were a few unexpected blow-ups in public, as when Bern without apparent reason slapped his wife.

It suddenly became evident that there were difficulties between Jean and Paul. Two months after the wedding, on September 6, 1932, Paul Bern killed himself; a bullet shattered his brain.

The suicide note left near Paul's body stunned and shocked the world. The wording seemed cryptic. The construction seemed confused. Bern's note threw no light on his suicide. It revealed nothing to the general public:

Unfortunately this is the only way to make good the frightful wrong I have done you and to wipe out my abject humility. I love you. You understand that last night was only a comedy.

For years Hollywood puzzled over the mystery of what he had meant. The public believed that Jean and Paul were happily married. What comedy did Paul refer to? What had he meant about a *"frightful wrong?"* What terrible thing could have happened to cause Paul Bern to feel it necessary to take his own life?

There was no question about the fact that Paul had killed himself. Yet in the previous weeks there had been no hint that Paul had reason to be depressed. Even the very day he ended his life he had seemed perfectly normal. He'd been at the studio that afternoon and gone home to do some work there before joining Jean at her mother's home.

When Jean heard about Paul's death she was reported to have come close to a nervous breakdown and actually attempted to kill herself in a moment of overwhelming grief.

John Carmichael, Bern's butler found Paul's body, on July 6, in the morning. Bern was laying on the floor, between the dresser and the bed, a gun in his hand.

According to Jean's report of what had happened on that tragic weekend, she and her husband had eaten at the home of Willis Goldbeck. The next day they had gone to, the studio. It was Paul's suggestion that Jean go to her mother's place to stay the night because she had to be at the studio the next morning. The next day, after work, Jean returned home and had dinner with Paul and then at his suggestion went to her mother's again, since *"My stepfather had gone fishing over the weekend, and Paul suggested I go over to my mother's because she'd probably be lonesome."* Bern said that he'd be there later. The police asked Jean if Paul had seemed all right, and she'd answered with *"Well, he complained of a bad headache, but he said it was because he'd been reading scripts all day. But he didn't seem overly depressed."* Paul never went to her mother's and it wasn't until the next day that she learned why.

Harold A. Garrison, Bern's chauffeur filled the police in on some of the other activities of Paul's over the weekend.

On Saturday Garrison had taken Paul to the M-G-M studios, where at 6 p.m. he had a haircut. Then Paul was driven back home, giving Garrison instructions to pick him up at nine on Sunday morning. When Garrison arrived the next day the butler told him that Paul was still asleep. The chauffeur waited until four in the afternoon. His employer never showed up. Garrison said: *"Carmichael went upstairs and came down to tell me that Mr. Bern was still asleep and that he couldn't get any sense out of him except that he wanted me to come back Monday morning."*

The only clue that gave any evidence that Bern had been considering suicide was brought out after long investigation. Many friends admitted having conversations with Bern on the subject.

John Gilbert said:

> The circumstances surrounding the incident are too delicate and too close to my heart for me to discuss them now. But it was at a time when Bern was deeply in it, and only then, he would turn his thoughts to Suicide. He was extremely sensitive. He would brood for days over some imagined slight.
>
> The ordinary pleasures of life meant little to him. He had become philosophical in his thoughts on death and eternity. He said to me once, "My only reason for living is the opportunity to give others happiness. Should the time ever come when I believed I am no longer able to do that, I will not hesitate to snuff out the candle."
>
> Paul Bern was my best friend. And if he thought that this was the time for him to go, it is not for me to criticize him.

Others told much the same story, and with such people like David Selznick, Louis B. Mayer, backing up Gilbert's statement, it became evident that Paul Bern had been thinking about doing away with himself for a long time.

A close relative was asked about the note left by Paul Bern and that person claimed that the man was simply apologizing to Jean for the suicide. Possibly pointing out that any man who would marry a girl and then kill himself had every reason to attempt, in some way, to excuse himself to his bride. This was only one possible explanation but surely didn't reveal much, nor satisfy the police or the public.

When the coroner's inquest was held, a Dr. Jones, who had flown in from Honolulu appeared and claimed that Paul's reason for killing himself was "acute melancholia." He said that he would give Coroner Frank Nance a clinical report on Paul, who had been his patient for the last six years.

The information Dr. Jones announced was highly confidential and privileged and he wasn't in a position to make it public. He told reporters:

> I am sure this will up the case and show, as impossible, the theory that any other person was involved in Bern's death. Bern suffered from a condition where trivial things which became exaggerated in his mind and resulted in acute melancholia. I know that his act was a personal one. I think I can prove this to everybody's satisfaction.

At the time, the doctor was referring to the false theory that it might be possible that Paul had been murdered—caused by a report that a car had been heard pulling away from the Bern driveway.

Whatever was in the doctor's report has been kept secret to this day but it apparently seemed to have proof, beyond a doubt, that Paul Bern had good solid reasons of his own for killing himself.

Two to three days after Paul's death George C. Clarkson, a Los Angeles insurance man, claimed to have knowledge of an early will of Bern's which made a woman by the name of Dorothy Millette his sole beneficiary.

A relationship which Paul had kept over the years, partly out of the idea that he owed Dorothy something for the years they had known each other, now came to plague Jean Harlow. Then the full story was exposed. It was discovered that Dorothy was in California, and had been in a San Francisco Hotel at the time of his death. She had come to Los Angeles around the time of Bern's marriage to Jean, apparently in the hopes of getting more money from Paul. The clerk at the Algonquin in New York said she'd left for Los Angeles a little before the marriage, but she wasn't officially heard from until after Paul's death. A San Francisco hotel clerk reported that he'd received a check made out to "Miss D. Millette" with Paul Bern's signature. Then the news began to gather together and it all come out about Paul having paid Dorothy's bills at the Algonquin for years, and that he had made it a habit to visit her every time he went to New York. There were even insurance policies that were to be paid to Dorothy.

Jean Harlow showed no surprise at the news about Dorothy and claimed that Paul had told her about the woman. Jean's casual acceptance of the existence of Paul's long-time "kept" woman backfired later. Dorothy Millette drowned herself in the Sacramento River, three months after Bern's death. Dorothy's sister, Viona Millette, put up a court fight in an attempt to get part of Paul's estate based upon the fact that her sister had been living in a state of "matrimony" with Bern for several years.

Viona Millette was given $2,000 out of the estate, which had been willed to Jean Harlow. Jean got the remainder of the $48,000, which had been Paul's worth at the time of his death.

During the next weeks the public saw a grief stricken Harlow, who couldn't work because of her anguish over the loss of her bridegroom. It was some time before it became possible for Jean to appear in public, or start making movies. But slowly she showed signs of getting over the loss of Paul Bern. Her pictures were highly successful and she continued making one after another. She remained single until she met and married Hal Rossen, her third husband.

This was the story told to the world through the publicity releases handed out by the studio. According to Irving Shulman they *were* designed to hide the true facts which weren't revealed until the mid-1960s when Arthur Landau, her personal agent and friend, decided it was time to tell the world what he knew about Jean Harlow and the truth about her marriage to Paul Bern. Landau turned over all personal records on Harlow to Shulman, and then told the revealing "true story" about the famous actress. If Jean was as honest with Arthur Landau as the man claims and if Landau did reveal the full truth for publication, then what really happened was somewhat "shocking!" The following story shows a completely different picture of Paul Bern and the events surrounding his life and death. (It has been claimed that Landau somewhat colored the story to capitalize on the publishing craze taking place at the time Shulman's *Harlow* was written.) Hard truth or wild fantasy it does offer a starkly interesting explanation to the mystery of the man's death. Perhaps the truth is somewhere between fact & fiction. For it would have been impossible to feed complete lies to a clearly serious writer such as Mr. Shulman.

This is the picture that Landau offered of Jean Harlow's marriage to Bern. It is a fascinating explanation of why he killed himself. It also offers Landau's assessment of the suicide note that was found with his body.

It isn't a pretty or pleasant story, but it tells of a secret torment that, if true, must have motivated Paul throughout his life, and gives motive to his humanitarian actions to help others. It also shows the painful anguish and perverse actions that became the other side of Paul Bern, the side which, after his death, was hidden from the public in an attempt to save Jean Harlow's career.

The story, according to Arthur Landau, is that from the wedding day the Harlow/Bern marriage was finished. The reception was a farce held for the sole purpose of saving Jean's career. The marriage was carried on merely as a social front; *it was a completely sexless marriage*.

Adela Rogers St. John, in an article about Jean Harlow that was published in the February 4, 1951 issue of the *Ameri-*

can Weekly, was the first to give any published hint as the truth about Paul Bern's secret:

> Paul wanted to marry Barbara (La Marr)... She'd refused. The night she married Jack Daugherty, Paul tried to drown himself. Jack Gilbert and Carey Wilson saved him, but plenty [of] gossip swept Hollywood. It was then that Barbara told me what kind of person Paul was and why she wouldn't marry him.
>
> When Harlow announced her engagement to Paul, therefore, I was in a spot.... When I went to see her after her engagement was announced, I learned that Paul hadn't told her about himself. I told her.
>
> "Then it's true," she said, and began to cry. "Paul loves me as he says he does, for my mind..."

Miss St. Johns, in a 1932 article for *Liberty,* suggested that the statement in Paul's suicide note referring to a "comedy" had to do with a meeting with some other lady at the Ambassador Hotel on the night of his death. She wrote:

> Is it possible that she (Dorothy Millette) was really Mrs. Paul Bern and that her poor brain, already in the grip of dementia praecox, evolved some threat which menaced the happiness of Paul's new wife, and that Paul believed his death would render the threat ineffectual?

It was a good theory, and possibly might have explained his actions that night.

Now, let's start reconstructing what was supposed to be the real happenings surrounding the Harlow-Bern marriage, and examine some of the background which led to Paul's death.

Paul, according to Landau, went to a doctor shortly after the marriage, at the agent's insistence, for help. The report Arthur Landau claimed to have received from Dr. Sugarman at Paul's suggestion was the following:

Paul's teenage years were plagued by a tormenting knowledge that he wasn't like other boys.

It wasn't until Paul was thirteen that he became aware of this difference. This teenage period for any one is filled with frustrations, guilts, fears, inner questioning about life and the newly growing sex urges and changes in one's body. For Paul it was a time of personal anguish and fear that was the outgrowth of learning that he wasn't physically maturing as other boys his age were. He was by nature a quiet, withdrawn youngster, and now he went even deeper into himself as this slow awareness grew to his "difference." Other boys showed every sign of growing interest in girls, every physical sign of maturing, while Paul learned that, unlike them, he was physically retarded, developing slowly, if at all. At first he felt only a sense of guilt, then alarm as time went on, as the teenage years started to slip by with no outward signs of the same physical changes which his male friends were experiencing. According to the doctor's report, Paul even failed in the experimental sexual practices which boys his age succeeded in and from that time on he became completely physiologically impotent. His own upbringing in the Jewish faith, which taught that sex was a thing saved for the purpose of having children, helped to build this physiological guilt and strengthen his impotence.

His awareness of being different combined with strong guilt feelings and finally made it necessary to turn away from the social activities of his age group.

With a driving motive to never reveal his shameful secret to others, Paul turned toward the idea of a theatrical career—anything to get him away from gym locker rooms, where it would be necessary to appear naked before other people.

The determination to seek a way out of self-exposure by taking up a career in the theater became an obsession that finally convinced his parents to let him give it a try.

From that point on, Paul's whole life changed. He wasn't exposed to discovery. During this period he would have night and day-dreams concerning acts of boldness, much in the vein of the escape literature of the times. He was the hero of olden days, saving princesses from a fate worse than death, a world famous athlete, a strong and daring male adventurer who could conquer the world with one hand and save a woman with the other.

Paul Bern was obsessed with the image of being a romantic hero, a dream which, in adult years, certainly accounted for his romantic and idealistic attitudes towards women and especially with Jean Harlow.

It has been suggested that Paul was a homosexual. But his life in the theater, where such relationships might have been easy to get into, gives every indication that the same physical lack of interest in women was felt toward members of his own sex. The only contradictory or difficult to understand fact, in light of the doctor's report and the statements which Arthur Landau made about Bern's marriage to Jean, is Paul's long-standing affair with Dorothy Millette with whom he was living in New York. That Paul lived with Miss Millette as husband and wife would suggest that he was certainly carrying on an affair. Or their relationship was something else, not involving a sexual intimacy. Yet his actions and statements before and after the marriage to Jean Harlow would give every indication that he and Dorothy had a sexless association. As Dr. Sugarman was supposed to have stated, Paul Bern was physically and physiologically unable to have sexual relations with a woman. Possibly at this early age he tried and partly succeeded with Miss Millette, but during his forties—while in Hollywood—he had become completely impotent. Nobody, but Dorothy Millette, could have given an answer to this. Maybe she herself was uninterested in sex and the two had found a very rewarding companionship in living a romantic existence without the necessity of sexual congress. Surely it was easier for a struggling young actress—especially if she wasn't very interested in sex herself—to be living with a man, who would do everything he could to support her, than living by herself or with another woman where expenses would be at least split. Miss Millette's emotional instability became evident by her actions after Paul's death.

Again, according to the Landau report, Paul said that while he was living with Miss Millette he became convinced that he might be a homosexual, since it seemed the only logical explanation for his inability to have satisfactory relations with a woman. This would indicate that the Bern-Millette affair was a sexless one.

His desperation at this age is illustrated by the admission that he had gone to great lengths to become sexually excited and thus prove that he was merely under-sexed. He read all the pornographic books he could get a hold of, looked at every pornographic picture he was able to find. In the end he even went to the famous "circuses" which were put on for people wishing to observe all the forms of perversion imaginable. Such places would go to all lengths to satisfy their customers. Presentations showed not only both men and women, in heterosexual and homosexual roles, but also examples of intercourse with animals, sadistic and masochistic acts, of whippings and mass orgies, all acted out on the stage in bright lights for all to see. But even this had no effect on him other than to make him violently sick and shamefully guilty.

The agony and torment that a man in his position would be forced to go through under these difficult conditions, certainly makes it understandable that it was possible for Paul Bern to do some of the things he was accused of doing to Jean Harlow on their wedding night. More than anything else in the world, Paul wanted to be normal. It became not only an obsession but also almost an emotional *perversion.* There is nothing worse for a man than to discover that he has *no* sexual feelings. Being gay may have been far less agonizing than being sexually dead. A person would feel they had not only been cheated by life, but that God Himself had turned against him.

When Paul arrived in Hollywood he honestly felt there was reason for hope in that this was the one place in the entire world which attracted the most beautiful and exciting females. His marriage to Jean Harlow, the very symbol of sexual excitement, the dream woman of America, may very well been at least partly motivated by the belief that she would finally manage to do what all others had failed: prove him a man with normal sexual feelings and desires.

Irving Shulman, in his Harlow biography makes and interesting quote in reference to Paul's personal torments, and is directly connected with his failure with Jean Harlow:

Every man—I know gets an...erection... just by talking about her. Arthur, didn't I have the might to think Jean would help me at least that much...? So why did she fail me?

While the public believed that Jean Harlow and Paul Bern were a happily married couple, and that even the motion picture Industry believed that everything was working out smoothly for them, the events revealed by Arthur Landau tell a completely different story. If what Arthur knew had been made public it would have been one of the biggest scandals to hit the Hollywood scene in years and both the Harlow and the Bern careers would have been finished.

What supposedly happened after the newlyweds had been left to themselves after the marriage would have been for Jean one of the most shocking and painful experiences that a bride can experience.

Jean wasn't completely innocent when she opened her arms for her groom's love on the wedding night. She had been married before, although her first marriage failed. She knew a lot about sex and what she had every right to expect from Paul. Arthur claimed she had never had relations with any man other than her first husband, but was sophisticated enough, both by personal experience and by exposure to the Hollywood scene to know the score.

This is very difficult to believe; though it could have been true. Many reports have claimed that she lived a somewhat wild life, enjoying many lovers. But such rumors and whispered gossip may have been nothing more than the fantasized stories circulated to titillate the public.

In either case, Jean Harlow was not a virgin and certainly not sexually naïve.

Paul appeared in the bedroom with words of love, and in his struggling attempt to find a way to approach his lovely wife, was in the process of kissing her feet when Jean suddenly burst out laughing.

What a horrid shock to a man in his emotional/mental condition!

Jean was young, and to a certain extent one must accept the fact she was a little innocent to the workings of the human mind. She knew from Adela St. Johns that there was little reason to expect much in the way of a satisfactory sexual union with her groom, but apparently had no idea of how sensitive a man like Paul could be. Possibly she reasoned that a man his age—in his 40s—was sophisticated enough not to expect too much, either. She could hardly know that he might have hoped that the "Jean Harlow"—sexy blonde bombshell—would be able to magically solve his life-long failure to respond to a beautiful woman. Her laughter at the very moment when he needed help, understanding, gentleness was cruel. Surely she was not fully aware of the possible resulting pain. But Paul had put all his hopes in Jean's magic ability to turn men on. Surely he must have believed she was laughing at him, at his body, at his actions.

What followed were certainly not the actions of an emotionally sane man. Nor were they the actions of the same man who had lived for the good he could do for others.

Paul was drunk. He had been drinking all day, and had reached an emotional point where everything centered on a successful act of love with Jean. His hopes, his every nerve and thought was tense and fired with an impossible and unrealistic fantasy as to the magical power of the nationally famous "hottest woman in the world."

In considering his acts one has to evaluate his mental and emotional attitude at the moment when Jean laughed at him. One has to take into account the fact that he had told many people and proven by actions—that he lived for what good he could do for others. One must consider why such a man, who was surely in love with the woman, who had always gone out of his way to be kind and generous, could suddenly turn into a raging sadistic animal. Unable to control his urge for revenge, control his disappointment and hurt, control the emotion they came erupting out of the very inner core of his frustrations.

In so considering and understanding the emotions and anguish, which moved Paul, there is no attempt to excuse or lessen the unforgivable actions of the man. To understand is not to excuse. To understand is not to forgive, but rather to see the honest and realistic motive behind these actions of an emotion-crazed man who suddenly saw his hopes crushed *in* the mocking laughter of a woman who had no way of knowing the full effect of her automatic act.

Paul went into an insane rage. Taking his cane, he proceeded to unmercifully beat Jean Harlow's back. The full extent of the damage done to Jean Harlow as reported by Arthur Landau was damning. Jean called him late on the wedding night, crying and begging him to come and get her. When he had brought her to his home, she pulled down the robe she had been wearing. Five long vivid welts marked her back. One of the welts just over her kidneys was marked with blood blisters.

Later it was revealed to Arthur that she also had a large bloody bite on her stomach and ugly bruises along her thighs.

Landau claimed that the only thing which kept him from going to Paul Bern's house and killing the man was the realization of what this could do to Jean's career. He insisted that the wedding reception be played out. And, as a face saving act, have the marriage continue for a length of time. This was to keep from ruining a career that had taken years to fully develop.

Before the reception, Jean was taken to Dr. Sugarman who examined her and did what he could for the young actress so she could go through with the reception. It was learned when Jean died that Bern's beating had damaged her kidneys, and that this beating was directly responsible for the sickness which took her life.

Arthur was the first man to discover Paul's long kept secret. Holding down his personal feelings, Arthur returned with Jean to the Bern home the next morning and discovered Paul lying naked on a rug in his den. Bern was face down. So it was not until Arthur turned him over on his back that he was aware of the truth of Paul's physical under-development. Everything from the waist down was no more matured than that of a small boy. Even the man's hips were delicate and boyish.

Arthur was attempting to sober the drunken man, whom he had now taken into the bathroom, when Jean came storming in. She wanted to take personal revenge on Paul for what he had done. It was then that she revealed to her agent the condition of her stomach and thighs.

Later, somewhat sobered, Paul was ready for the reception.

Everybody who knew of the true situation did fine acting jobs. Nobody else guessed the truth. The newly married couple played the young lovers completely and convincingly. When it was all over it was the belief of the Hollywood community that Harlow and Paul Bern were a happily married couple.

During the next days, in which Paul made no attempt to touch Jean, things moved smoothly enough. Jean went to Dr. Sugarman for care and finally Arthur convinced Paul to see the doctor.

Sugarman's final medical opinion concerning Paul Bern was that there was nothing he could do for the man, and that Paul's only hope was to get psychiatric care. The doctor explained that it was doubtful if Paul could ever have any kind of orgasm even in the process of coitus. Sugarman stated that though the man had some sexual feelings he was unable to achieve a substantial erection and it was therefore virtually impossible for him to enter into active coitus with any woman.

It now became obvious that Paul Bern, regardless of what he had done to Jean Harlow, was to be pitied more than anything else. Even Jean seemed to have managed some feelings of pity for him, in-so-far that they carried on a form of distant friendly relationship during their short marriage. It was a play they were acting out until they could get a divorce without damaging their careers.

The story that Arthur reported that Jean told about their last night together would indicate they had even managed to become strangely close. Sex had not become a part of their lives, yet the subject was toyed with.

It need not be pointed out that Paul's own reaction to what he'd done to Jean was as painful to him as to those others who knew the truth.

Yet, at times, events took place that again revealed the inner battle which was being fought within the man.

Once at a party Paul struck Jean, an act which seemed to have given him a sense of perverse power, a feeling of strength, a moment in which he felt, at least in part, like a man. That he did everything in his power to control this feeling, to control the temptation to repeat such acts, surely points out that he wasn't by nature a sadistic man.

According to Jean, on the Saturday night before Paul Bern killed himself, they had talked at length about attempting to somehow manage a sex life. Paul, had in the past—in an innocent attempt to find anything which might help him sexually—answered advertisements in pulp magazines which offered sexual devices designed to solve his very problem. He left the bedroom and then returned with a gadget strapped onto his hips, purporting to be a male sexual organ, commonly called a dildo. It was one of those objects that he had sent away for in the hope that someday he would find one that could solve his problems. What followed was a series of actions that might have been played by a clown. No attempt at any form of intercourse was made, but rather Paul played out a clownish mockery, as he danced around the bedroom, going through suggestive motions that convulsed both himself and Jean. It was a burlesque of the very things that he wished to be—a mockery of his own defects and failures.

Yet there was some reward to Paul, insofar that Jean, in her moment of laughter and reaction to his prancing antics, felt a tenderness and closeness to him at this moment. They slept together in the same bed, each filled with their own feelings of nearness and affection and understanding. But during the night Paul went out by the pool, alone and painfully aware of the mockery he'd played out, a mockery that was far sharper than Jean's laughter on their wedding night.

The above scene certainly gives one explanation to the postscript written on Paul's suicide note. *"You understand that last night was only a comedy."*

Even the rest of the note is easily explained by Arthur's account of the events surrounding the Harlow-Bern marriage.

"Unfortunately this is the only way to make good the frightful wrong I have done you and to wipe out my abject humiliation."

Now we come to Jean's attempted suicide, which was supposed to have been acted out in a moment of terrible and anguished grief.

The papers were filled with this suicide attempt, and it certainly made good copy to the fact that the marriage had been a highly romantic and rewarding one. Jean Harlow who had loved her husband so much attempted to kill herself in a fit of grief over the loss of her dear and beloved Paul.

Taking into consideration the above account that Arthur Landau revealed as the truth behind the Harlow-Bern romance and marriage, one finds it hard to believe that Jean would possibly have been so emotionally upset by Paul's death to attempt to kill herself. Of course it might be possible that she felt a certain amount of guilt, and in a moment of depression had actually been impulsive enough to not want to live with that guilt. On the other hand it doesn't really seem very reasonable that a woman in Jean Harlow's position, who had been merely playing out a farce until the right moment came along to divorce her husband, would have been all that upset.

Arthur's account of the suicide attempt seems far more reasonable.

According to this story, a close relative conceived and staged the whole thing, and had to actually force her into playing out the greatest piece of acting in her career.

Building on the events which Arthur Landau's story made public, the mystery of Paul Bern's death and suicide note become transparently clear, leaving nothing to the imagination. It accounts for everything. It reveals motive and understanding for events that have puzzled the public since the tragic end to Jean Harlow's second marriage.

Yet the most terrible implication is that Jean's death, a few years later, was caused by these very events.

But before she died, as an indirect result of the beating taken by Paul Bern and the damage caused to her kidneys, she became more than a mere living legend in the series of films which followed. She became also the pattern for the "blonde" sex symbol, which even Marilyn Monroe followed. Her style and her image made the sexy platinum blonde a Hollywood standard in such movies as: *Bombshell* with Franchot Tone, *Dinner at Eight* with John Barrymore, *Hold Your Man* with Clark Gable, *The Girl from Missouri*" with Lionel Barrymore and Franchot Tone, *Reckless* with William Powell, Franchot Tone, and Rosalind Russell, *China Seas* with Clark Gable and Rosalind Russell, *Riffraff* with Spencer Tracy and a child star, Mickey Rooney, *Wife Versus Secretary* with Clark Gable, Myrna Loy, and James Stewart, *Suzy* with Franchot Tone and Cary Grant, *Libeled Lady* with William Powell, Myrna Loy, and Spencer Tracy, *Personal Property* with Robert Taylor, and *Saratoga* with Clark Gable, Walter Pidgeon, and Lionel Barrymore.

Arthur Landau has certainly offered a possible solution to the mystery of Paul Bern, but one has to take into account several basic truths of life. How much of the real truth would a woman tell a close friend, no matter how close this friend might be? How many details will become confused and faded in long years? How much of the full truth did Arthur Landau actually reveal? What was colored, even inventively shaded?

What kind of story could a less emotionally deranged and guilt-ridden Paul Bern tell? How much different would that version be?

There is no attempt made here to doubt the detailed report made for Arthur Landau by the accomplished author, Irving Shulman. There is no question that the public was thusly given a chance to see one intimate account of Jean Harlow's experience with Paul Bern. What is the truth? Perhaps nobody will ever know for those involved are long dead. Speculation based on eye-witness accounts and public records can only offer a version, a selected conclusion created from highly limited facts.

The only ones who really knew the complete details of what actually happened, blow by blow, are now dead—Jean Harlow and Paul Bern.

Paul Bern left his story untold. This has been an attempt to see the working of his mind, the motivations, which must have moved the tormented man through life.

The mystery is still no more completely solved than it ever was. Only Paul Bern, himself, might have been able to strip the legend and scandal completely naked so that all eyes could finally see and understand. But why would he have done that, exposing himself to such humiliation and public shame? His death said all that he wanted to offer as his last living statement.

Jean might have shed some light to the darkness, and certainly she seemed to have offered a large amount to her agent and personal confidant, but her story was slanted, and incomplete. It is seen through the words of a third party. Even if she had "confessed" all one has to wonder just how much she might have subconsciously hidden even from herself. We all lie, concerning our lives. We all hide behind endless masks, deluding not only the public but also our inner selves. And people, like Jean Harlow, who become a product of Hollywood Big Studio PR departments, are nothing more than illusions, make-believe, images on a screen which reflect little of the real person under the skin. It is all makeup and clouded fantasy, play-acting that sadly covers over what is, in reality many times, nothing more than a tragic mockery of what actually exists under the surface.

But if everything offered here concerning Paul Bern's sexual problems is true—and how that was kept secret from his soon-to-be-bride until the wedding night—then their story is without question a classic argument for pre-marital sex. Or, at the very least, open honesty between two people before they enter into a marriage.

Ah, if things could only be ideal. But, of course, nothing is.

Paul Bern died with all his imperfections showing, with all his pain and anguish shadowed in a darkened mystery and accented in the vague last statement to the world, and thus created one of Hollywood's most intriguing puzzles.

Unsolved.

PART FOUR

THE THELMA TODD MURDER SCANDAL

Hollywood, once considered the glamour capital of the world, has also often been considered the scandal capital as well. Ever since the motion picture industry settled in this West Coast metropolis and became Big Business, all sorts of scandalous activities, including rape, dope addiction, and even murder have been mysteriously hushed up by one means or another in order to preserve the "good name"—and box office security— of the celebrities involved. And more than one Los Angeles District Attorney has yelled *foul,* claiming that the moguls of the motion picture industry have made pay-offs to hide, destroy, or distort the facts.

Often, even when the facts are available, high-priced lawyers are able to dance a legal tightrope and confuse a jury and witnesses sufficiently to defeat what originally seemed like a sure victory for the prosecution. Case in point being the O. J. Simpson murder trial, in which a vast majority of the public at large was outraged by the jury's conclusion that Simpson was guiltless of the double murder.

The jury system is the best we can have, but far from perfect; and flawed in too many ways. The guilty get off and many times the innocent are locked up for life.

It can be a nasty business.

But even then, the Hollywood scene has for decades been cluttered with scandals and even false issues brought before juries and judges, and most of all the public media which has always been able to crucify even those who are, in fact, innocent.

One typical example of this was the well-known trial involving Errol Flynn, who was charged with seducing two under-age girls. In this instance, a sharp attorney managed to prove that it was actually the girls who had committed the seduction—*not* Flynn!

And the term "in like Flynn" became a popular phrase with blunt sexual implications. It has become part of our language. Most people have no idea concerning its origin.

But far more prevalent than the actual trials of celebrities are the whispered rumors that can never be proven one way or the other. Undoubtedly you have heard and wondered about many of the typical so-called "facts" that even today still raise up their nasty heads to even clutter the Internet of the twenty-first century!

RUMOR: Band leader Glenn Miller is not dead, but is a basket case. *What a lovely thought for fans to embrace! This seems to be a truism: anything rather than dead!*

RUMOR: Actor James Dean is not dead, but is also a basket case. *Another case of flawed denial by "loving" fans.*

RUMOR: Silent star Fatty Arbuckle used a chunk of ice in the performance of an abnormal sexual act on actress Virginia Rappe, which resulted in her death. *Which ruined his career! And he was found guiltless!*

RUMOR: Carol Landis committed suicide because a famous star had made her pregnant and then refused to marry her. *Oh, my, aren't we the lovely worshippers of female morality!*

RUMOR: The Frank Sinatra, Jr. kidnapping was nothing more than a publicity stunt. *As if that kind of stunt was needed by the Sinatra family.*

RUMOR: The medicine which caused Robert Walker's death was given to him by his doctors—against his will. *Well, okay, all right, it is possible for doctors to do many a questionable deed! But give us a break, will ya all?*

RUMOR: Actress-comedienne Thelma Todd was a dope addict.

Okay, we can stop here and look at the facts!

Of all these and other rumors concerning Hollywood celebrities, some are true, some are smoke screens deliberately propagated to confuse the *real* facts, and some are merely the product of wild imagination and envy. And therein we find the confusion, the tempting madness which the media just loves to feed upon. They aren't interested in facts so much as charming and audience to their commercial voice, be it on paper, film, radio or TV, cable and satellite. The media fights for their share—as large as possible—of the vast public greedily seeking entertainment! And the tabloids of the world are crammed with half-lies and distortions and sometimes just fantasy. *Two-headed alien gives birth of the new Ice Creature with five stomachs and a web foot!* That's sure to grab an audience waiting in line at the local market's check stand. And some of these classic rumors are as foul and unrealistic, or clouded in hocus-pocus flash phrases to catch the eye. One-liners. Sound bites. And the Internet! Where will it all end? And how do we divine truth from lies?

In the case of Thelma Todd the truth will never be known; and her untimely death will remain one of Hollywood's most talked-about mysteries for decades to come.

The coroner's jury publicly labeled Thelma's death as accidental; yet everyone connected with her death that had the courage to speak up felt that she must have been murdered! Most vile; most commercial; most exciting headlining! Or was it the truth?

Let's look at some of the facts and illusive beliefs that came out of the investigations.

As with virtually every scandal involving Hollywood personalities subsequent to the establishment of the Hays Office, in Thelma's case the evidence was so clouded over, the supposed facts so contradictory, and the investigation so casual that the real truth behind her death was never satisfactorily explained.

Whether the movie Industry had made pay-offs to conceal scandalous facts, or personal friends of Thelma's had kept quiet in order to save her reputation, or both parties contributed equally, will probably never be discovered. But the small amount of available evidence clearly indicated that some person or persons unknown had done everything possible to deliberately confuse the facts and conceal the true cause of this young beauty's death.

At least that's one way to look at what is actually known or not known. Another way would be to suggest truth is stranger than fiction or rumor or tabloid reality.

When such confusion and distortion of available evidence makes it impossible to arrive at a clear-cut conclusion regarding these mysteries, it is almost a necessity to examine the various rumors whispered about them, since all too often at least one of these rumors may be the real truth, originally told in confidence, but slowly passed on from friend to friend until it leaks out to the general public.

In the case of Thelma Todd, the mystery which surrounds her death makes it definitely appear that she *was* murdered by some unknown but probably influential assailant. And in checking the so-called evidence against the many rumors regarding the cause of her death, it would appear that the rumors offer far more reasonable explanations for her death than those which the movie officials, the newspapers, and the local authorities would wish the public to believe!

Thelma Todd was one of the few actresses who were fortunate enough to successfully make the transition from silent films to the "talkies." Starting as a young comedienne opposite Laurel & Hardy, Buster Keaton, and other top silent comedians, she quickly caught the public's fancy as a light-hearted glamour queen comparable to Jean Harlow and Carole Lombard. Had she lived, she undoubtedly would have become one of Hollywood's top female stars. Yet, had she never gone into motion pictures, she might lived a full life into the 1960s or later.

Like so many others in the movies, Thelma Todd was "murdered" *by* Hollywood—not directly, but by association. The Hollywood environment, which allows individuals to be put upon pedestals and literally worshipped until they feel they can do no wrong, is the culprit for putting these emotionally vulnerable actors and actresses in a state of eventual self-destruction. Thelma's suicide—or murder—is only one example of this, with such names as Wallace Reid, William Desmond Taylor, Carol Landis, Lupe Velez, Gail Russell, James Dean, and Marilyn Monroe being only a few of countless others.

This is not to say, obviously, that Hollywood will cause

the self-destruction of every celebrity who embraces the bright lights of this glamour capital, or that Hollywood is an evil in itself. However, there is no denying that the entertainment industry—which is virtually synonymous with Hollywood—is an extremely high-pressured business involving millions of dollars which utilizes the services of sensitive artists who by their very sensitivity are emotionally fragile and therefore subject to the dangers that such competitive pressures bring to bear on their psyche.

For this reason, Hollywood can be a "killer" to the type of creative artist who cannot cope with these emotionally difficult problems of survival.

In recent scandalous headlines, we have read about motion picture and television stars who have become alcoholics, drug addicts, sexual perverts, murderers, and marital musical chairs experts. Yet Hollywood today doesn't begin to compare in terms of pressure to the city it was in the golden era of the Cinema of the twentieth century.

In the Twenties and early Thirties, Hollywood was a closed society, a glamour center far more complicated than it is today. The star system was just beginning to establish celebrities of international renown. There were heroin dens in Chinatown, speakeasies, bootleg booze, wild parties and wild living. Any performer caught up in this uninhibited social climate was bound to be changed by it. To make the temptation easier for these stars, the adoring public felt they could do no wrong—and the studio bosses made sure that the public kept believing the lie.

And how sad that things never got better. Over the decades the dope venue became an international norm that has created major power blocks which are so that they almost own countries. But even in the early twentieth-century drugs of any kind were there to be had, if you simply knew the right people and had the money. She had the money and knew the right people. And more importantly had the kind of addictive personality that would drive her right into a life-style destined for self-destructive behavior. She lived on the edge, tempting fate.

For Thelma Todd, a woman who loved living and lived with every nerve in her body, the Hollywood social whirl was a deadly temptation...one that presumably led her to eventually become a narcotics user!

This part was not fiction. It was pretty much an accepted reality in her life.

There is no doubt that Thelma was the center of attention for at least one of the many Hollywood in-groups. She had the beauty and wit to captivate even the most bored veteran of the glamour capital. And she was going places fast. Little did she know just how fast and to what untimely end she was going as a result of being this center of fun and frivolity!

She was born in Massachusetts, a state far enough away from the film capital to have her career as a Hollywood star seem extremely remote. She grew up in a relatively happy environment which had little to do with motion pictures; and completed her formal education with a college teaching degree.

The only episode in her early life even vaguely connected with her later career was the winning of a teenage beauty contest that gave her the title of "Miss Massachusetts."

However, at that time—unlike so many other beauty contest winners—Thelma had no aspirations for an acting career. She wanted to be a teacher, and bent all her efforts in that direction.

Probably she had never given any serious thought to acting as a career. Of course, the idea could have crossed her mind, as it would any beautiful young girl of the time; but she had been raised by a father deeply interested in politics, who apparently taught her to be practical and realistic. Acting was a form of day-dreaming and therefore not proper for people who based their life on reality. On the other hand, teaching was a practical profession, a logical and honorable career for Thelma to contemplate.

But dreams sometimes have a way of winning out over logic; and perhaps this is what finally happened in Thelma's case, because when the opportunity came for her to pursue a career more glamorous than teaching, she jumped at it. And in view of her intelligence and shrewdness, chances are that she had something to do with the existence of that opportunity!

Thelma was a beautiful young woman with blonde hair who was definitely country club material. She certainly would have been the life of any party in high society had she married some young executive and settled down into a normal social environment—which she originally expected to do.

But she was also highly independent with a strong desire to be on her own, to make her own way through life. This willingness to stand on her own feet was demonstrated when she worked as a fashion model in order to go through college without her parents' financial support.

Her work as a fashion model apparently didn't immediately influence her thinking regarding an acting career. During this time, it was obvious that she centered most of her attention at college to obtain a teaching degree, with no other apparent ambitions in mind.

It wasn't until her first year as a sixth grade teacher that her ambition changed direction...towards Hollywood.

There is no hard evidence that Thelma deliberately planned to campaign to become a star. But once she decided to change her ambition in life, it is probably safe to say that she at least to some degree became a dedicated self-promoter.

Perhaps she initially merely attracted the attention of the right man: a theater manager. Perhaps she had been playing up to this man and he saw the chance to impress a beautiful young girl—and reap the rewards. Then again, perhaps he merely saw a potential star whom he felt should be called to the attention of the proper studio officials.

In any event, the manager of a local theater sent a picture of Thelma to Jesse Lasky, suggesting that she be in the movies.

Beautiful as she was, however, Thelma was no more photogenic than hundreds of other young women who were eager for fame and fortune in films. Therefore, there was no apparent reason for Lasky to bother signing her to an immediate contract merely on the basis of her good looks. She was an untrained beauty, nothing more. What possible acting talent she might have was unknown, untried, untested. But Lasky saw that subtle *something* in Thelma's photo that spelled potential star material. He wrote to her, offering her a place in a school for young actors in Astoria, Queens. Paramount, Lasky's studio, at the producer's urging, had created the school as a means of finding potential star material and training it to the point where it could be exploited for full commercial value.

It is difficult to know his real motives, but what can be known is what followed.

The fact that Thelma needed only the letter from Lasky to send her packing to New York City is strong indication that somewhere deep inside her was the suppressed desire to become a glamorous figure, rather than merely a colorless school teacher. Can one blame her? Everybody has an ego wanting to be stroked and admired and fully developed. From the moment she received Lasky's letter, teaching was part of Thelma's past; acting was her present and her future and her end.

New York was a new, strange world for Thelma, but she blended in eagerly and easily. Her winning personality, her well-endowed figure and her beautiful face made her immediately popular.

The acting school proved to be six months of grueling study, heart-breaking effort, learning about make-up, etiquette, dramatics, costuming, dancing, swimming, automobile driving, fencing—in effect, anything and everything which might be of some value in the roles a motion picture performer might be required to play, as well as being an aid in the general development of poise and grace.

Thelma and twenty-three other young hopefuls endured these months of rigorous training with only one ambition driving them day after day to exhaustion: the dream of stardom.

Finally, at the graduation dinner given on March 2, 1926 at the Ritz-Canton Hotel, sixteen of the most promising men and women were given a one-year studio contract as a reward for their effort—and as the first major indication that they were truly potential stars.

It is impossible to underrate the sheer joy and excitement this tangible reward must have caused amongst the lucky sixteen winners.

And for Thelma Todd, whose name was on that list, it must have been the happiest night of her young life. At last she was on the first step towards her goal! She knew only too well that ahead lay even more hard work, more grueling hours, days and weeks. It would be months of struggling, hoping, and maneuvering before she could achieve the next step on her road to stardom. But her dream was beginning to become a reality, and she had the beauty, brains, and determination to see it through!

For most young hopefuls, the first year contract is the most crucial. During that brief period of time, the unknown performer must in some way become sufficiently popular with the studio and the movie going public to warrant the renewal of the option. If a performer remains relatively unknown by the time the year is over, their option is almost never picked up, and any career is finished before it has begun, because now it must be started all over again at the bottom, angling for some means to obtain a new studio contract. For most young performers the emotional strain is too great to endure more than once. In such a way the weak are weeded out, and only the very strong and determined have the chance to make it up the next rung of the ladder to possible fame. Even then, timing and chance and luck all blend together in a terrible series of lucky breaks that are haphazard at best. If any element is missing, failure is assured.

Fortunately for Thelma and the other fifteen fledgling stars, Paramount, unlike many of the other studios, was not only willing to gamble on training unknowns and give them contracts, but was also willing to give them an immediate opportunity to display their talents in current productions. Thus, instead of each performer having to connive for initial roles in films by playing up to veteran producers, directors and/or stars on the Paramount lot, they could rely on the studio to provide them with the chance they needed to make good. Without the pressure of the Casting Couch game.

Someone at the studio came up with the idea for a movie entitled: *Fascinating Youth,* in which a part would be written for each of the new contract players. Of course, none of these parts would be very long or important or demanding, but to each of the sixteen men and women it represented the chance of a lifetime! They were in pictures! They were getting their first chance to prove themselves, to see if they had that intangible magnetic glow that spelled the difference between *star* and *performer.*

In spite of—or because of—presenting sixteen new faces to the public all in one motion picture, *Fascinating Youth*

111

did reasonably well at the box-office. Today, it might be compared to the typical teenage musical B movie or your standard TV youth movie. But the times were different in the Twenties. Then, rather than worrying about the competition of television, motion pictures were the prime entertainment medium for the general public. Movies were produced on the assembly line, exhibited for a small admission price, and thus available to virtually everyone who wanted to escape to the dream world of the celluloid factory.

Regardless of what critics today might say about Thelma Todd's performance in *Fascinating Youth,* at the time she made a sufficiently impression on the studio officials to have them give her subsequent roles. And it is interesting to note that of all the unknowns trained at the short-lived Paramount acting school in Astoria, only Thelma and one of her classmates ever achieved fame. The other classmate, who later became the husband of America's sweetheart, Mary Pickford, was none other than Charles "Buddy" Rogers!

Thelma's hard work at the acting school was finally paying off for her. On the screen her personality came across with a naturalness that brought her one role after another in silent films.

Then, suddenly, the entire motion picture industry was turned topsy-turvy by the release and overwhelming success of a non-silent film, the first "talkie": *The Jazz Singer,* starring Al Jolson!

What television did to Hollywood in the forties and fifties is nothing compared to what the "talkies" did to the movie capital at that time! The entire movie industry was geared to silent film production, a special form of entertainment demanding certain acting and directorial skills especially suited to story-telling in pantomime.

But with the advent of the "talkies," not only did the voice become suddenly important, but a whole new set of directorial techniques had to be developed. Many artists, both in front of and behind the camera, found that their careers, which had been perfectly secure during the silent film era, were suddenly at an end. Sometimes it was because they were unable to adjust their techniques to the new requirements. Sometimes, particularly with matinee idols, it was because the public felt that the voice, heard now for the first time, did not match the mental impression of what that voice *should* sound like, based on the public's conception of the star during the silent era. (One is instantly reminded of the wonderfully amazing satire *Singing in the Rain*, which dealt directly with this kind of vocal problem! It tells a story of Hollywood in transition, with Gene Kelly and Donald O'Connor dancing it up with a young Debbie Reynolds. A truly classic film and musical!)

In the beginning, however, "talkies" hurt the Hollywood producers more than it did the stars and directors. Millions of dollars worth of silent film productions had been completed, awaiting release dates—and now they were all totally antiquated!

Of course, the first "talkies" like *The Jazz Singer* were little more than silent films with a few scenes added in which dialogue or songs were introduced via synchronized records played in the theaters. Sometimes the sound didn't quite match the lips on the screen, particularly when the film print had been spliced, thus throwing it permanently out of synchronization with its accompanying sound track recording. But the audience didn't mind. This was an exciting new novelty: pictures that talked! And the public screamed for MORE! The Hollywood studios shook to their very foundations as a result of this clamor for *more* and *more* talking pictures! Each studio lost not only its financial security based on the completed silent productions it had expected to release, but many of the top established stars and directors of each studio proceeded to fall out of favor with the public, leaving a dangerous hole in the box-office potential of each new production! To fill this void, new stars had to be discovered and exploited immediately! Old stars had to adjust—or fade away.

It was during this hectic period that many supporting players from the silent era who had good speaking voices became stars, while many stars whose voices handicapped them in some way became merely supporting players.

Thelma Todd was one of the lucky ones. She was able to make the transition from silent pictures to the "talkies" smoothly. And being available for talking roles during this difficult period gave Thelma an important boost in her career at a most propitious moment.

Surprisingly enough, even though her previous acting experience had been limited to the six months' training she had received at the Astoria school, Thelma developed quickly into a highly capable performer with the kind of magnetic appeal that guaranteed her popularity with the movie going public.

Now she was *really* on her way!

Her personal life was every bit as successful at this time as her career. Men flocked around Thelma, giving her the pick of the most handsome bachelors and playboys the world had to offer. She took the choice cuts!

Thelma was a highly passionate young woman with the kind of body that attracted men of all ages and all walks of life. And to Thelma a relationship with an attractive male didn't stop with hand-holding and kissing. When she saw someone who appealed to her, she didn't bother to be coy. Her personality was such that each opportunity in life for fun, excitement or business was an opportunity to be exploited to its fullest degree of satisfaction.

Who knows, maybe there was something within her that felt life was short and she had to gather as much of it as possible in as swift a time as possible. Some might believe this theory. Most realists would simply suggest she was a woman out of control, flying at high speed towards disaster. She was an additive personality. Today we have all those 12-Step programs, but even AA hadn't been invented back then. Thelma was a woman on the fast track, determined to get the fully value out of her living experience.

There is no official record of her sleeping her way up the ladder to fame. There are no conclusive facts to point Thelma out as the type of easy-virtue starlet who would climb into bed with the nearest studio executive who might be inclined to give her career a boost. No casting couch player here! But such means of gaining a more secure foothold in Hollywood are the rule rather than the exception, especially since each new year brings hundreds of new faces and figures, all a little younger, a little more eager than the previous year's crop, all willing to do almost anything for a start up that ladder to stardom. It takes a certain amount of hard-headed realism as well as talent to become a star in Hollywood, and if sleeping with the right man helps, why not, some say. Well, so long as the starlet enjoys sleeping with men, what's wrong with sleeping with those men who can do the most for her?

As for Thelma, according to all reports, she was a woman who grabbed hold of life with both hands and shook out of it everything she could get. Perhaps she was essentially a thrill-seeker at this stage of her life, a girl riding a glittering Hollywood merry-go-round, enjoying every minute of it, with no thought of the ride ever stopping. Perhaps her ride to the top was so fast, so dream-like, that it dazzled even her levelheaded personality. In any event, she seemed to search for a meaning of life in the arms and beds of her handsome suitors. And the rumor that she lived a good portion of her life in Hollywood "hopped up" on narcotics would surely give the impression that she was either deeply insecure or desperately in need of experiencing every kind of "kick" Hollywood had to offer.

Thelma was quoted as saying: *"While we're here we should laugh, be gay, and have fun."* And she certainly did her best to live up to this philosophy, no matter what her real reasons for doing so might have been.

Her appearance in a wide variety of motion pictures during this time was making her a top Hollywood personality.

She was cast in almost every kind of film: westerns, mysteries, dramas, melodramas, comedies, and even musicals. And with each successive role she continued to impress Hollywood and the movie going public with her charm and versatility.

But it was in comedies that she became most popular.

Anyone who remembers the early sound classics starring the Marx brothers and Laurel & Hardy can never forget the tall blonde beauty named Thelma who was the perfect foil to these cinema clowns. She was a young woman with a sharp sense of timing that caused many experts to praise her as one of the top light comediennes in the field!

A series of comedies in which she co-starred with Patsy Kelly was so successful that the public kept screaming for more! It was perhaps comparable to the Ma and Pa Kettle series which was so popular with the general public in later years, in terms of its zany, down-to-earth, rib-tickling humor.

All in all, Thelma Todd performed in over seventy motion pictures before her untimely death at the age of thirty.

Strangely, with all of this fame and glamour, with her tremendous popularity, with men flocking from far and wide to win her attention, Thelma was a woman who became obsessed by ever-increasing fits of depression. It is hard to imagine that such a young, beautiful, talented, and obviously successful woman could be anything but happy. Everyone who was close to Thelma was impressed by her outgoing nature, her bouncy, vivacious temperament. From all outward appearances she seemed to be the picture of health and happiness, a woman who was in complete control of her destiny.

But all of us are a complex mixture of opposites. Those of us who are outwardly gay are often secretly depressed. It is very possible that today she would be diagnosed as manic-depressive or bipolar.

Perhaps she had gained fame and success too quickly, too easily. Perhaps life seemed to hold no real challenges for her at this time. Some of her friends have suggested that this may have been the underlying problem for her restless, outwardly gay, inwardly depressed nature. But a closer look at her life, her career, her basic personality, reveals a far more tragic possibility.

Hollywood, like any other successful big business, attracts the underworld element. Many a top star has been accused of being boosted to fame through the influence of the underworld. A typical example is George Raft, who admitted that his beginnings in Hollywood were an outgrowth of his underworld connections.

At the time Thelma Todd was a Hollywood celebrity, the movie capital was surrounded by criminal elements. There were prostitution and Chinatown heroin dens, to name only two obvious examples. This was during Prohibition and bootlegging was a socially, if not legally, accepted crime across the nation—and the movie capital made no effort to hide the fact that it sanctioned continual wild parties flowing with bootleg booze.

A popular fringe element was the underworld gangsters

that ran most of the night clubs, or at least had their fingers tampering with any place that sold illegal liquor. These men were as interested in Hollywood glamour as the rest of the nation. Some claimed that even Joe Kennedy was a connected personality who circulated in this crowd. Considering the questionable support for the anti-liquor laws which were finally overturned, one can simply wonder who was right and who was wrong. Nice respectable people made big money in the liquor business before and after this period, and some low level underworld men like Al Capone profited as a result of the illegality of the booze business. Obviously such power brokers as the Kennedy's were easy meat for nasty rumors. And surely Joe was famous for having come to Hollywood to back and produce films and gather into his influence people like Gloria Swanson, who was credited as being his long-time mistress during these years. The good and the bad, the decent and the criminal level swam around the Hollywood social circle.

In fact, her connection to such people is suggested by the following which has been rumored as fact:

It has been reported that she was involved with Charles "Lucky" Luciano, the famous gangster known to be violently dangerous, who had his hands in just about every possible illicit business. Supposed he helped to get her hooked on drugs. Like all rumors, one has to decide what to believe. She certainly was known to enjoy the company of many men. But the part of this rumor that fascinated is what was reported to have taken place at the famous Brown Derby one night. In an argument involving Luciano's request she let him make use of one of your rooms at the Roadside Cafe she own, Thelma was supposed to have exploded: "Over my dead body" His reply was classic: "That can be arranged." An almost too cute a story to believe. But as they say: truth is stranger than fiction—or even pop rumor.

The pay-off here, of course, is that there is much rumor about mass pay-offs to keep the facts concerning her demise in an eternal cloud of mystery.

One ends up wondering: If the Luciano story is true, then it may have been possible that he lived up to his threat. Yet he was never seen in Hollywood—which doesn't suggest he couldn't have hired somebody. Still, perhaps, too pat.

Yet it is the underworld connection to show business and drugs that certainly is suggestive of almost anything being the actual truth. The problem is that all the theories are painfully possible.

And the Luciano could certainly have been a part of any drug connection.

It was not difficult, therefore, for a woman of Thelma Todd's beauty and charm to capture the interest of the top figures in these dubious fringe groups. The repeated rumor that she was a dope addict certainly suggests that she had some sort of "working arrangement" with those underworld figures who could obtain for her the illegal drugs. And although no facts or specific names are hard evidence, nor just rumor, it can be assumed that Thelma might well have socialized with men like Luciano, who, at the very least, had strong contacts with the underworld, and who, perhaps, deliberately got her started on dope in order to keep her under their influence. And the Luciano story touches on those elements in spades.

When and where Thelma became involved with the taking of narcotics is difficult to ascertain. But that she was ripe to enter this level of escape is evident by the way she acted in her last years.

In the beginning, however, when she was first on top, still living an exciting and hectic life as one of Hollywood's most promising young personalities, the only narcotic she needed was love. It was during this time that she met a man by the name of Pasquale Di Cicco, who was a theatrical agent.

Pat Di Cicco and Thelma seemed to hit it off immediately and explosively. In July, 1932, with virtually no warning, they eloped, marrying in Prescott, Arizona.

On their return to Hollywood, they repeated their marriage vows in front of a minister in Los Angeles. One gets the impression that here were two young impulsive people, both with a zest for life, who ran off to get married in a flurry of romantic impulse; then, wishing to make their marriage bonds all the more binding on their return home, repeated them in solemnity and humility.

Sadly enough, their enthusiasm soon faded. What exactly was responsible for the break-up in their marriage is difficult to determine. The fact that both were highly romantic, attractive, and surrounded by too many temptations certainly added to the crumbling of their marriage. That they still were emotionally involved with one another became evident in the last couple of days of Thelma's life—some time later. But both Thelma and Pat were the type of people who had lived by their guts far too long to be happily settled with one, lone, imperfect human being.

On March 3, 1934, Thelma Todd sued for divorce on the charges of incompatibility and cruelty. Like so many events in Thelma's life, far too little is known about the true reasons for this action.

During the following eight years Thelma continued to make pictures in Hollywood, eight years of fairly good success. But she was all too aware of the fact that very few actors or actresses last long in the motion picture industry.

Movie history is filled with stars who made a million, only to end up in the poor house, And Thelma Todd was intelligent enough to realize that her career would not last forever. So she started searching around for a safe business in which to invest her money.

For Thelma it turned out to be a restaurant located north of Santa Monica on the coast highway. Roland West, a man who had directed pictures in the past, went into the venture with her; and the two of them lived in separate apartments on the second floor of the restaurant; indicating, apparently, that they were *not* involved in an intimate relationship with each other.

Beside Roland's apartment, he had a bungalow up on the hill above the restaurant which had a large garage, where he let Thelma park her car. But beyond this courtesy and their business relationship, they lived their own separate lives.

The fact that the restaurant was a success proved the soundness of Thelma's investment. But the need for such an investment seemed unnecessary, considering that her movie career was going better than ever.

From all outward appearances, things could not have been better for Thelma Todd. Yet the truth was completely the opposite. Fame had brought on other experiences which she had to live through; experiences that must have been harrowing to

119

her, considering the way she acted.

Again, it is necessary to fall back on what few facts are known and try to piece them together into a logical picture:

There is no detailed public information concerning why Thelma Todd might have been the victim of blackmailers or extortionists. There are many possible theories, of course, many implications to deal with, but none of these are undisputable fact.

The rumor that she was on dope probably began at this period in her life.

Her constant fear of being followed, fear that "gangsters" were after her, or about to kidnap her, were not completely a product of her mind. On at least one occasion a man *was* actually arrested on the charge of attempting to shake her down for money.

Her chauffeur reported that Thelma would many times tell him to drive faster because she was convinced someone was following them.

Since no facts actually came out after Thelma's death to give evidence that she was actually in danger, other than the cloud of mystery as to the real cause of death, it is necessary to consider the fact that Thelma might have been at this time a narcotics addict. If this were so, it is highly possible she had gotten involved with a Hollywood element that had no connection with the motion pictures, and that she could not get out of their clutches.

If one is to believe the claims of her lawyer and the statements made by some of the coroner's jury that Thelma Todd had been murdered, it surely would fall in line with her own fear for her life.

Something, obviously, was frightening Thelma Todd during the last months of her life; *something* that caught up with her and was directly responsible for her death.

These mysterious events all began to come to a head in December, 1935, the month of her death.

It is interesting to note that a now famous actress and director, Ida Lupino, played an indirect role in the last known hours of Thelma's life.

Ida, the daughter of Stanley Lupino, a comedian of that

era, was unknown then as an actress, but she was responsible for Thelma's last public appearance in the social whirl of the Hollywood movie colony.

Ida and her father, Stanley, friends and admirers of Thelma, planned a party in her honor at the Trocadero Restaurant.

An event which took place before the party might have some bearing on Thelma's strange death, since it was made an important point by the people involved:

A couple of days before the party, Ida met Pat Di Cicco, Thelma's ex-husband. He had heard about the party and wondered why Ida had not invited him.

Miss Lupino explained that she had merely thought it might be embarrassing to both himself and Thelma if he were present.

Di Cicco was quick to inform Ida that he would be delighted to come, so she did the only thing left and invited him.

If an argument can be the cause for murder, or if there was more to the argument than met the eyes and ears of those present at Thelma's party, the invitation to Di Cicco could have some bearing on Thelma's death—but only if…!

Di Cicco arrived at the party with another woman, ignoring the fact that a special seat had been saved for him next to Thelma. And things blew up—sky high!

According to one witness questioned, Thelma went over to where Di Cicco had seated himself at a table some distance from her own, and really laid into him. Even Ida Lupino claimed that Thelma "berated him bitterly" for having slighted both herself and the hostess.

Yet after the blow-up things seemed to have simmered down, and Thelma showed every evidence of having enjoyed herself. When she left some hours later, Thelma was in a gay and happy mood.

At her rented limousine outside the Trocadero, Thelma turned, waved, and said in a mockingly solemn voice, *"Goodbye!"*

No one realized how prophetic that statement was going to be!

Hollywood had honored her with a party, and now she was waving her last goodbye to the city that had given her fame and fortune—and soon an untimely death!

It is not hard to imagine the thoughts which went through the minds of those present at the time, when they learned of Thelma's death.

Could she have possibly have known that death was near at hand?

Did she plan to kill herself?

Did she know that someone was planning her death?

Nobody can know except Thelma.

Ernest 0. Peters, the man driving the rented car which took Thelma home that night, claimed she told him to drive faster because she was frightened and believed that somebody might try to kill or kidnap her. This would give evidence that Thelma's last goodbye had been meant to be just that! Though that does sound somewhat melodramatic and difficult to believe.

The amazing thing about Thelma Todd's death is that there was so much evidence, even in her own words, to suggest murder as the cause of her death; yet nothing serious was done in way of investigation. The very *lack* of investigation seems to indicate far more completely than anything else that in her case, at least, there were pay-offs made somewhere along the line for some mysterious reason.

The following facts certainly show that there is every reason to believe that Thelma Todd *was* murdered, and that the evidence was distorted to protect the killer—or killers:

About four o'clock in the morning, Thelma Todd was driven up to the front of her restaurant, Ernest 0. Peters offered to walk her up to the apartment, since it was so late, but she made it a point to tell him not to bother. Usually, he would be requested to do this service for her, yet on this night she flatly refused to let him. *Why?*

Was she expecting to meet somebody? A secret lover? Or did she have to deal with something more threatening, like a blackmailer?

Shrugging away his surprise, Peters drove off, leaving Thelma standing alone on the sidewalk.

As far as the *official* record goes, this was the last time anybody saw Thelma Todd.

Other witnesses claimed to have seen a woman looking like her. One witness purported to have received a phone call from her; but Thelma was never seen again under such circumstances as to convince the police it was, in fact, Thelma Todd. Though there was every reason to believe that Thelma was actually alive that Sunday morning and afternoon.

Some twelve hours later, around 4:00 p.m. Sunday afternoon, Mrs. Wallace Ford told the police that she had received a call from Thelma. The Fords were giving a cocktail party that day, and Thelma was calling to say she was planning on being there. According to what Mrs. Ford was quoted as saying that Thelma told her, the actress planned on bringing some man with her who would make Mrs. Ford "drop dead" with surprise. *Who that man might have been was never revealed.*

More evidence as to Thelma Todd's activities on this last day of her life was offered by a druggist. He told the police that a blonde woman, dressed in evening gown and fur jacket, had come into the drug store to make a telephone call. This was about the same time that Mrs. Ford received her call. *The druggist claimed under oath that it was Thelma Todd.*

Later, at 11 p.m., another witness said that a woman who looked like Thelma Todd came into his tobacco shop and asked to make a phone call. He was dialing the number for her when she suddenly turned and rushed out. Stunned, he watched her walk down the street until she met a man who was holding a fur coat. *His description of Thelma's evening gown matched that of other witnesses.*

Jewel Carmen, the estranged wife of Roland West, Thelma's restaurant partner, saw Thelma in a car with a strange man she did not recognize.

She had known Thelma for a long time and there was no question of her ability to recognize the young actress.

These three events, plus other evidence which came into focus, strongly indicated that Thelma was *not* killed on Saturday evening, as originally thought, but probably late Sunday night.

She did not appear at the Ford cocktail party.

As to the man she was seen with on Sunday, there is only a slight clue as to what he looked like: One witness who had seen him said that he was dark and foreign-looking. Nothing more. That might suggest Latin, Italian, or Spanish. It could mean nothing.

If the man in question had anything to do with her death, there is no real evidence to prove this theory. He was never found; he never offered himself as a witness to explain Thelma's activities during the day.

However, this points a finger fairly strongly to the fact that he *could* have had something to do with her death! A man who had been with a woman who is found dead the next day would normally be expected to appear before the police to give any information he could. There are very few reasons for *not* doing so:

One: He was involved in Thelma's death.

Two: He was frightened, though innocent, possibly because of underworld connections.

Three: He was dead himself.

Four: He was a pick-up and did not actually know whom he was with.

The last is difficult to believe. That he was dead himself seems questionable, because surely there would have been some investigation as to such a man's death, and the information thus found could easily be connected in some way with Thelma Todd. That he was either guilty of Thelma's death or had information which might have been dangerous to himself or friends, is possible. There is even a fifth possibility for his reason not to appear before the police; *somebody paid him off.*

Now to the hard facts surrounding the discovery of Thelma's body and the aftermath of that discovery:

Thelma Todd's maid, on reporting for work Monday morning, discovered that her mistress was not in her apartment. She saw that up on the hill the garage doors were open. She climbed up the 270 steps and, walking into the garage, discovered Thelma's dead body.

The actress was in her car, slumped over the steering wheel. Her face was utterly covered with blood.

There was blood splattered all around Thelma, on the seat, and running board,

The strange thing was that there were no signs of struggle. Thelma's evening gown and fur jacket were untouched—in perfect condition. If she had been attacked, her clothing should have been torn and ripped from her body.

According to so-called expert reports, this was good reason to believe that Thelma had actually killed herself. But it could just as easily be explained by claiming that she had been murdered elsewhere and then taken up to the car, to make it appear to be suicide.

The fact that the police department started a complete investigation when they first arrived at the scene at ten in the morning, and then suddenly, without any apparent reason, did not follow through, surely suggests that certain influential powers pulled political strings to hush up the true facts of Thelma's death,

Anybody who saw Thelma's body in the car was certain that she had been murdered.

Thelma's mother, the police who arrived that morning, the grand jurors, all felt there was every reason to believe that the actress had been killed.

Yet later, Mrs. Todd, Thelma's mother, claimed that the death of her daughter was accidental!

Everybody else also reversed their original opinion.

But Thelma's lawyer continued to believe that the young actress had been killed.

Somebody was making threatening sounds, making pay-offs, and *almost* everybody was listening.

Why a mother would be willing to remain silent to the murder of her daughter, how she could be bought off, is hard to guess. It can be suggested that if the truth had been revealed, Thelma's reputation after death might have been so terribly ruined that her mother favored silence to justice. Possibly she was even convinced by others that Thelma had actually died accidentally.

But let us examine the facts further:

Thelma did *not* walk up the 270 steps from the restaurant to the garage, which was first suggested by the fact that she was found in the car, dead.

Investigation proved that her evening shoes would have shown some kind of scuffing after such a long walk—and there

125

was no such scuffing!

The official record is clear as to what the police decided should be the "facts" of the case:

Upon autopsy, evidence was found that carbon monoxide poisoning had been the cause of Thelma's death.

The fact that there was so much blood on Thelma's face was explained by claim that, in passing out from the fumes, she had hit her face on the steering wheel.

One of the theories which surely was far more logical, taking into account all the evidence which was available to the police concerning both Thelma's death and her past life, suggested that she had been hit in the face, then placed in the car.

The murder *might* even have been unpremeditated.

Possibly she had an argument with the dark, foreign-looking man, which continued into a fight. He picked up some heavy object—or used his fist—and hit her.

Maybe he panicked. realizing that she was dead, and then put her in the car in an attempt to save himself and make it look like suicide,

It is equally possible that she was deliberately murdered, although no motive was evident—other than her contacts with people who might have given her narcotics, and her fear of being blackmailed or kidnapped,

The police at first suggested that Thelma had left her house key in the apartment that day and, upon discovering her situation, returned to her car and started the engine in the hopes of warming herself. But the fact that she could *not* have walked up and down the 270 steps without scuffing her evening shoes ruled that theory out.

When they had ruled out their first logical theory, the police immediately turned toward Thelma's many love affairs,

It was brought out that Thelma was interested in a new man who could not appear at the Lupino party given in her honor because he was out of town at the time. The name was never revealed—possibly it was the same man whom witnesses claimed to have seen with her on Sunday afternoon.

Di Cicco had argued violently with Thelma at the party, but it hardly seemed logical that he would thus have sufficient motive to kill his ex-wife. If they had gotten together afterwards, on Sunday, for some reason and had another argument, then a fight, it could have been unpremeditated murder. This would also supply a logical reason for Thelma having claimed that the man she was bringing to the Fords party would knock Mrs. Ford off her feet. Surely nobody would have expected to see Thelma with her ex-husband as escort. If this was true, and Di Cicco did accidentally kill her, he might have been the man who placed her in the car to make it look like suicide.

What exactly caused the investigation to peter out can only be guessed at. Payoffs were the most logical motive, taking into consideration what happened some time after Thelma's death.

When the coroner's jury finally gave a verdict of accidental death, which Thelma's mother publicly announced to also be her belief, Deputy District Attorney Johnson suggested otherwise. He believed Thelma had killed herself. He was quoted as saying:

"It seems too difficult to believe Miss Todd went to that garage and started the motor of her car to keep warm."

Yet, Patsy Kelly, who had co-starred with Thelma in several comedies, publicly announced that she did not believe Thelma would have killed herself. They had been very close friends for years, and her opinion can be accepted with fairly good authority. She said that Thelma had had everything to live for: fame, fortune, love and life. Thelma, according to Patsy, had *no* reason in the world to kill herself!

This, and the fact that Thelma's lawyer was convinced it was murder, surely suggests that what evidence was made public was merely a smoke screen.

Some three months later, an event took place which leaves little doubt that the truth behind Thelma Todd's death was purposely hidden, that for some unknown reason *someone* was making sure that nothing was done to expose this truth! Because of this, it is hard to believe anything other than that Thelma Todd was murdered and that big money had paid for silence!

The Los Angeles Police Department received a telegram from Ogden, Utah, which had been sent by a well-dressed, middle-aged, black-haired woman—unnamed—claiming she had evidence that Thelma Todd had been killed and that the man who had murdered the young actress was in Ogden. A man's name and hotel address was given, and all the police had to do was investigate. It was also stated that the man had taken up residence at the hotel after the death of Thelma Todd,

Someone intercepted the telegram. It is impossible to know who that *someone* was. But!

Fact One: the woman sent the telegram.

Fact Two: the telegram was *not* answered.

Fact Three: the telegram was *never* made public by the Los Angeles police!

It was the Ogden police who did an investigation on the basis of the telegram—but *not* through the orders of Los Angeles. They learned about the woman and the telegram, and then did their own private investigation.

What they discovered caused Police Chief Rial More to contact mayor Harmon Peery. Neither the police chief nor the mayor had reason to become involved with a farce or mere imaginative rumor. The fact is that these two men, holding high offices, having nothing to gain from making a big noise without purpose, contacted the Los Angeles police, stated what they had found, and reported that the man in question should be immediately investigated in connection with the death of Thelma Todd,

The clincher is simplicity itself:

The Todd case had been closed, The Los Angeles Police Department had no further interest in the subject. As far as they were concerned Thelma Todd had, at worst, killed herself. That was it!

Finished!

The amazing thing is that *nothing* was done! The questions are endless,

Why?

How could the authorities get away with *not* making at least a routine investigation?

What had convinced them so completely that there was *no* reason to believe that Thelma Todd had been murdered?

Where was the pay-off—if any?

Had Hollywood been so completely thorough in a series of pay-offs as to make it literally impossible for anybody, no matter how politically important, to do *anything* about Thelma Todd's death?

Or did her death involve far *more* than mere murder of a young actress?

Who was being saved?

Hollywood? Los Angeles?

An influential gangster?

Or was there some other implication, never even hinted at?

It is hard to believe that a police department as big as that of Los Angeles could be paid off.

It is hard to believe that somebody would not have done some investigation on this new evidence offered from Ogden.

Is it possible that Police Chief Rial Moore and Mayor Harmon Peery were merely making up stories to gain national attention?

Is it possible they were merely grabbing onto a straw for free publicity?

Hardly!

Is it possible that the Los Angeles Police Department had some evidence which made it impossible to do anything against the man in Ogden—because they already knew about him, and purposely ignoring his existence?

Is it possible that Thelma Todd might have been murdered by some foreigner who had diplomatic immunity—or to involve him would be to involve some foreign nation into a scandal which was not worth gaining so-called "justice"?

Nothing more was discovered about the man in Ogden. Nothing more was discovered about Thelma Todd's "dark and foreign-looking" male companion.

It is interesting to let the mind wander, to speculate on all the facts, to extrapolate them to the furthest extent.

Why did her mother believe it to be murder and then change her mind? Fear of something? Was there really reason to believe that Thelma Todd had killed herself or died accidentally? Or was Mrs. Todd attempting to hide some far more terrible scandal involving her daughter?

Why didn't Thelma appear at the cocktail party being given by Mrs. Ford? She had planned to, and she was apparently alive during the time of the party.

Who was the man she was with? Somebody impressive, no doubt, from what Mrs. Wallace Ford said.

Why didn't her male companion appear before the police to give what information he had on Thelma's last day alive?

It *is* possible to accept accidental death! It *is* possible to accept suicide! But it is *not* possible to understand why these above questions have never been logically answered!

Her fear of being kidnapped, murdered, blackmailed, might have been for the most part the product of an over-active imagination. But then why was one man arrested and questioned for having tried to shake her down?

And the question of Thelma Todd being a narcotics addict: Where does that fit in—if at all?

Too many questions. Too little facts. The implications can be endless.

Nonetheless, one simple fact remains: *Thelma Todd died under very questionable circumstances; the police investigation which started with a bang, whimpered out; and not all the evidence was carefully analyzed.*

Not all the questions were answered—and far worse, most of them were not even allowed to be asked!

It has been suggested that Hollywood made key pay-offs. And surely this could be possible. But it is just as possible that the pay-offs could have come from somewhere else.

Where?

That is one of the questions not allowed to be asked!

Maybe her death was much like the death of Glenn Miller, James Dean—nothing more than what was made public.

Maybe to say that Thelma Todd was murdered is no more sensible than saying that Miller and Dean are basket cases.

People will believe what they want, People will look at the evidence and see only what they desire to see, make out of it what intrigues and satisfies their own imaginations.

Personally, the evidence examined here makes the author believe there is every reason to say that Thelma Todd was murdered in cold blood, that the unknown killer escaped, and that the investigation—for one reason or another—was never complete enough to reveal the *real* facts of the case.

Hollywood, or some *body,* created the smoke screen which even to this day is so thick that it is impossible to see through clearly.

Thelma Todd is another personality in the Hollywood legend whose life ended in a cloud of mystery—and it is anybody's guess as to who was responsible!

PART FIVE

LANA TURNER'S FIGHT WITH HER DAUGHTER

Columnist, George Sokolsky wrote in the New York Journal-American:

> Cheryl Crane, the little girl of too many fathers, is a sad girl who could have had everything but who had nothing. A girl who spent her childhood and girlhood watching a procession of lovers and husbands wander in and out of her mother's bedroom and to whom the sight of her mother being physically abused by men became an everyday occurrence. She is a girl who learned about life, long before she understood what she was learning.

Her story, twined around that of her mother and father, certainly illustrates the important impact of a childhood environment. What happens to us at this point of our development will effect later years and even our sexuality. Sometimes parents can offer wonderful shelter, love and caring, while others have been accused of child abuse, which certainly damaged their children's adult years. The list is long with famous names. Marilyn Monroe was a victim of childhood rape, which had a distorting influence over her adult years. Judy Garland was dominated by a studio head who fed her pills in order to keep her functioning during tight schedules of filmmaking. Rumors that many child actors and stars were victims of dominating parents, even sexually abused by them, are common media fodder. Joan Crawford's daughter claimed that the famous actress was a brutal child-beater and a somewhat horrid mother. Nobody is without sin; nobody goes through childhood without some nasty business to twist and pervert their later years. Even today, with super stars such as Michael Jackson, we hear rumors and stories about childhood abuse that may or may not be true.

We aren't interested in the truth of such rumors so much as the fact that some events reported in the media illustrate the public's feelings, bias, and sense of right and wrong. And, of course, many of these stories contain enough truth for readers to take them seriously.

As a prime example of how early childhood experiences can be responsible for later tragic events, the story of Lana Turner and her daughter, Cheryl Crane, is bluntly illustrative. Nobody can know the truth other than the survivors. And they, generally, will be reluctant to expose the totality of their experience. And, even truth is sometimes tainted by bias.

It is enough. By simply examining the following material one can realize how such childhood experiences can have tragic fallout in later years.

Lana Turner was one of those Hollywood stars who played a free-wheeling game of high living to the hilt. Lana, who never seemed to know the meaning of money, spent it as if there were no end to the supply. She lived in a mansion which consisted of two dozen rooms, including a private beauty parlor and soda fountain, located in the expensive Brentwood district of Los Angeles, near Santa Monica. The home had a king size swimming pool with a cabana almost as large as an apartment house, equipped with massage machines, sunray lamps, hot and cold showers, and a supply of bathing suits for as many as a dozen guests. There was air conditioning and a loudspeaker system in every room of the house.

Lana had her own projection room, which reportedly showed films far more racy than those for which Hollywood had become world famous. The house was a showplace for the Hollywood crowd, where parties turned into what were reported to be wild orgies that included nude swimming parties for her thrill-seeking friends.

She had a $25,000 silver service that could accommodate sixty guests. She placed a dozen phones around the rambling mansion for the convenience of her guests. Fresh flowers were delivered every day of the year.

She even went so far as to buy a fur-upholstered Cadillac, which she turned in a couple of weeks later, at a loss of close to $2,000, because she suddenly decided she didn't like it any more. And in the mid-1900s money went a lot further than it does in the twenty-first century.

She lived as if tomorrow would never come, and therefore, she felt as if she had to make the most of today.

At M-G-M Lana had a dressing room that was more of a luxurious apartment on wheels. The room had coral-colored sofas and chairs placed on deep plush rugs, a refrigerator, range, record player, color television set and a ten-foot dressing table. It was the envy of every actress on the lot, and when one top female star demanded one just like it, Lana threatened to top the studio by buying one so expensive and large that it would be financially embarrassing for them to match it. Her need to have the biggest and best of everything was an obsession.

Lana's fourth husband, Lex Barker of Tarzan fame, did everything he could to control his wife's excessive spending, but to no avail. At this time she was making $5,000 a week, forty weeks a year.

But the squandering of money wasn't the only Turner weakness. The most powerful and obsessive weakness was men. The depth of this obsession for men is suggested by a story circulated in Hollywood concerning herself and a bartender.

According to the story, she was with an escort at one of the Sunset Strip restaurants when she met the bartender. Lana managed to get rid of her escort and ended up spending the night with this new acquaintance. Hollywood gossip columnists claimed that this affair raged so high until it became too dangerously embarrassing for Lana. At that time, Lana was still married to Bob Topping, the millionaire playboy. Even if this story were pure fictional media gossip, it fit the image which the public had Lana Turner.

A year and a half later, Lana called her bartender boy friend and invited him to her Palm Springs home for the weekend. When he arrived, according to his report, not only was Lana there in a revealing negligee, but another of Hollywood's hottest feminine stars, Ava Gardner, was also present and was similarly dressed. He was invited to learn the mysteries of what made Ava such a popular hit with men and then allowed to favor Lana with the same intimacies.

Another report, which circulated through Hollywood concerning Ava and Lana, was that they were not only close friends and willing to share the same male partner. But that they had, in fact, found time to enjoy each other in the same way (a story not denied even when published in a national magazine). It must be pointed out that in Hollywood any whisper becomes rumor and any rumor suggested firmly enough is accepted as fact. Nobody could ever say that either actress lacked a healthy desire for the opposite sex; so one is left to draw their own conclusions, regardless of a lack of denial.

Nonetheless, the fact remains that Lana Turner, one of the hottest things to hit the movie screens in her time, was thoroughly confused and frustrated in her personal love life. Not only confused by herself, but by a daughter, who constantly got in the way of her private affairs, purposely attempting to cause trouble between Lana and her lovers.

Lana's life and story is that of a woman possessed with a driving need for romance and male companionship. She was fickle and never satisfied with one male companion for any long period. She "fell in love" with any lover who was more than casual. In the moonlight she found it very easy to love, and in the cold light of day she cooled off. Her romances were public property. She was the hottest thing to hit Hollywood bed land. She admittedly didn't know the true meaning of love, believing that a physical attraction was the only thing necessary to be "in" love. Her marriages to date number five, all failures. The famous men with whom she became involved during her love career read like a list of Hollywood Who's Who—Male Department.

Frank Sinatra, Fernando Lamas, Tommy Dorsey, Howard Hughes, Rory Calhoun, John Dali, and the late Tyrone Power were but a few of her off-screen lovers.

Artie Shaw, Steven Crane, Bob Topping, Lex Barker and Fred May served their time as husbands. And Johnny Stompanato elevated the Lana-Cheryl murder scandal into the international papers, shocking the world and almost completely ruining both women's lives.

Yet in all fairness it must be said that no woman would consciously bring on herself the continued romantic failures which Lana Turner had always suffered. Regardless of the sordid life that surrounded Cheryl Crane's childhood, her mother's continued changing of male partners, it isn't fair to put all the blame on Lana's shoulders. Nor is Lana totally responsible for the life which the daughter began living when she grew old enough to be out on her own.

Sure, it is easy to point a finger and say that no mother has the right to openly play around with any man who attracts her. "Keep your private life private! Don't give your children a bad example!" these moral preachers would demand.

It is easy for some to claim that Lana Turner was nothing but a tramp, that she had no respect for morality, that she couldn't have cared a damn about her child or the role as mother. But a realistic view of Lana Turner's love affairs, and her constant habit of changing male partners, may be to realize that they were caused by circumstances, at the time, beyond her control; that she was caught in a living trap.

Some people feel that no mother who really loved her daughter would live the kind of life Lana Turner did. It seems pretty clear when closely examining her career and life that she was a woman fully aware of her own faults, painfully torn with feelings of self-guilt, and terribly hurt by her failure to be a good mother to Cheryl.

It is so easy to over-simplify a person's life, to gather together limited facts to paint a nasty picture. It is, also, all too easy simply to take the glossed over, pretty picture events and paste them together to create an ideal, unrealistic image.

The truth, in reality, is something far more complex. None of us is merely one thing: We are a wild mixture of good and bad, idealistic and monstrous. But we generally live somewhere in-between those outer limits, hiding away the rough edges, the haunting, and nightmare parts. We try to survive in a world, which is vastly complicated with invisible landmines. Many don't survive. Most are scarred and damaged by events impossible to avoid.

Life, itself, is a maze through which none of us ultimately survive.

Many of us barely manage to make it through each day without experiencing terrible emotional crises. And being a parent brings on even greater traps and confusions for some—even more demanding responsibilities. Some people are ideally suited to be parents; others aren't.

And even under ideal conditions of love and care, raising a child is, at best, difficult and challenging.

Cheryl's childhood, marked by a series of step-fathers and a financially irresponsible mother, was not a firm foundation for nurturing a normal adulthood. At best this kind of experience will be difficult, if not seriously damaging.

Louella Parsons and others believed that Lana Turner was a woman who, having entered motion pictures at the age of sixteen, did not mature emotionally until later in life. For years Lana was an emotional teenager in her reactions toward men. She fell in love quickly. She was in love with love. Physical attraction and sexual need combined in her mind, to equate with love. But no matter how immature Lana might have been in her understanding of genuine love, she developed in "sophistication" insofar as living the wild life, Hollywood-style. Knowledge came slowly and painfully through blundering mistakes, which changed an innocent young teen-ager into a worldly woman. And much of this came through a series of casual affairs.

Lana Turner's story certainly reveals abundant evidence that the rumors about her affairs weren't merely the fabrication of gossips. Lana, herself, pointed out the underlying reason for her personal failure as a woman and, therefore, a mother when she said:

"Maybe it's all been too easy. Maybe that's what's been wrong."

And surely her rise from literally "rags to riches" came easily for Lana Turner. She was born, according to the best evidence, in 1921 in Wallace, Idaho, the daughter of an itinerant copper miner.

At nine, living in Modesto, California, she worked as a scullery maid. On Christmas Eve she lost her father, when thugs robbed and killed him. This unexpected and tragic loss had its effect on Lana throughout her life. From that moment on, Lana was convinced that she was different from other children, and in her adulthood still fought desperately to convince herself that she was as normal as other people.

One story is that Lana, as a teen-ager, spent a year in Hollywood trying to get any kind of job that would be offered to a girl her age. Then, one day, as Lana sat in Schwab's drugstore not far from the high school she attended, a man named Mervyn LeRoy walked in, looked at her already beautiful face and figure, and, on the spot, offered her a movie contract.

Now, that sounds just like a movie fantasy! And to some extent, it apparently was.

Of course, whether it happened that simply or not is unimportant. Lana was, regardless of any stories claiming otherwise, *officially* discovered in Schwab's drugstore while sipping a soda. It is true that such "discoveries" are usually a fiction of some studio publicity writer hiding the fact that the person discovered had been a long-standing friend of a talent scout or studio executive. The truth was more interesting: it was at the Top Hat Café, across from Hollywood High, that the publisher of the Hollywood reporter saw her. She was advised to call the Zeppo Marx agency (Zeppo being one of the famous Marx Brothers). This, plus the man's personal introduction to Mervyn LeRoy became the start of her film career. Legend claims that Lana, at fifteen, was at the right place at the right time. As a result of this, she was offered a role in the film, *They Won't Forget.*

According to her official website, she was born Julia Jean Mildred Frances Turner on February 8, 1921. A name which director Mervyn Leroy felt was just not right. He was the one who suggested Lana.

Thus Lana Turner was born!

Normally years of hard work, effort, pain and tears and thousands of dollars are required to bring a struggling young actor or actress to the attention of Hollywood VIPs.

Lana Turner, with a background of childhood tragedy, suddenly found herself, overnight, projected into the world known as Hollywood in its hey-day. Stars were the gods and goddesses of this world, worshipped, adored, treated like royalty, living like kings and queens in a social kingdom of their own making.

Lana soon became romantically interested in Gregson Bautzer. He was the first man of importance to enter her personal life. Bautzer was a lawyer of some reputation and often so occupied with his profession that it was impossible to find time for Lana. She was "in love", though some of those around her believed it to be nothing more than puppy love and surely in light of what followed, it must be accepted that this was the case.

They were romantically linked for some time in the papers as well as in private life. The newspapers and even her mother were convinced that marriage would soon unite these lovers.

Lana, at this time, was making a picture with Artie Shaw, the famous clarinetist and bandleader who became notorious for his many marriages and romances. There was no secret about the fact that they didn't hit it off at all. Lana, according to her mother, hated the man.

Then came the night when lawyer Greg Bautzer was tied up with business affairs and Lana was left without an escort.

In Lana's own words, as reported by Louella Parsons, this is what actually happened:

> I had a date with Greg and he called to say that he couldn't keep it. Some kind of legal business. I got mad and decided I'd go out anyway and I thought of someone who'd make Greg mad—and jealous. So I called Artie...about midnight Artie said it would be nice if we got mar-

ried. I said it would be nice, too. The next thing I knew, we were on our way to Las Vegas.

From Vegas, Lana called her mother to announce that she'd been married, but one important fact she forgot to mention was that it was Shaw, not Bautzer, who was the groom. It isn't hard to imagine her mother's surprise when the next day, on reading the newspaper, she discovered that Artie Shaw was her son-in-law.

This marriage between two international personalities, with the low boiling points typical of artists, was doomed to failure.

The marriage did have one interesting effect on Lana, which seems to reveal, to a certain extent, a side of her character, at least during that period of her life. Artie, more mature and worldly than Lana, was the first to make any effort to expose her to the pleasures of good music and good books. Apparently, Artie enjoyed the idea of taking the still young and fairly unsophisticated Lana in his hands and molding her into a well-rounded woman. It appeared that Artie and his beautiful "gutter snipe" were trying to act out the script of George Bernard Shaw's *Pygmalion* But unlike Eliza in *Pygmalion,* Lana wasn't about to be remade into her husband's image of what she should be. Lana realized that she should have been interested in the cultural things Artie was trying to expose her to, especially since she hadn't received much formal education, but she was quoted as telling Louella Parsons that the books made her "sleepy." Apparently, Lana, now one of the top Hollywood box office attractions, already used to high living and spending, seemed to feel these reading assignments were too much of a struggle, considering that they certainly wouldn't contribute much to her bank account. Because of her indifference toward cultural pursuits, the relationship between Lana and Artie was severely strained. Lana felt that she did not have the time or inclination to give up more enjoyable interests for books and serious music.

After five months of exposure to culture, the marriage ended.

After the divorce, Lana ran wild, becoming involved with such Hollywood bachelors as Victor Mature, Turhan Bey, and Howard Hughes. Considering her reputation, there is good reason to believe that the involvements were more than casual. Lana was now riding high in her career, her pictures were extremely successful and there was little question that she could continue to remain on top as long as she wished.

Here was a woman who had grown up in a fatherless home, who had suddenly been rocketed into stardom, where some of the most exciting and glamorous men in the world were available as escorts. And yet, Lana was basically still a little girl responding to a concept of romantic "love" that only immature teen-agers believe in. She was having a ball in a world that revolved around her. No wonder she enjoyed making the most of this wildly exciting life. Hollywood had, for years, been selling the public on the idea of romantic love, of fairy tale romances, of Prince Charming and moonlight. Love was an image, a mood, and a fantasy of glittering colors. And Lana was enjoying this banquet of romanticized love and gathering as many samples as she could from the table Hollywood offered her.

Then one night in 1943, in a bar, she met a man named Stephen Crane. Some say she merely picked him up. But regardless of how it happened, this struggling, unknown actor made an impression on Lana that penetrated the giddy whirl in which she was involved. Suddenly she was head over heels "in love." Maybe it was merely because Stephen Crane fell hard for her and the other men in her life at the time hadn't been so serious. But there is one truly evident fact; after the first sputter of storybook stars, it was Crane who loved her the most.

One short month and another whirlwind romance developed into marriage. In a short time it became obvious that Lana wasn't as much in love with Stephen as he was with her. From the beginning, and for many years after, Stephen Crane had a strong personal affection for Lana Turner, and it can be said, in all honesty, that he hadn't married her because of her fame and position.

Two things happened in fairly quick succession to Lana and Steve Crane, one shattering and the other happily: both unexpected.

142

Stephen Crane, as it turned out, had been married before meeting Lana, and though having been divorced hadn't received his final decree. Oddly enough, this fact was apparently unknown to him. When he married Lana, therefore, he had honestly believed that he was legally free of his former wife. The news was like an earthquake to both of them. There was nothing they could do but have the marriage annulled.

No sooner was the marriage annulled than Lana discovered she was pregnant. There can be no doubt about the fact that it was a shocking blow to Lana.

Lawyers were quickly consulted in a desperate attempt to see what could be done about marriage, since both naturally wanted the child. After some legal shuffling it became possible for them to remarry. Stephen Crane was delighted. No one can question Lana's own relief—if not overwhelming delight—that things had worked out for them. It was hoped by both, that the coming child would hold them together, making their marriage the success necessary to create a happy family life.

Those who claim that Lana didn't want the child and that she was a poor mother who resented being burdened with a young daughter are merely victims of cruel, unfair, blind bias. What they aren't aware of is the fact that Lana was not only advised, but also urged, to have an abortion, because doctors were convinced that childbirth would kill her.

Nobody can accuse her of not wanting the child or of being a shallow and hopelessly selfish woman. Under similar circumstances thousands of women have quickly taken a doctor's advice, a very understandable and intelligent decision.

Lana chose to take the chance, regardless of the risk involved, because she wanted the child. This, in spite of the fact that marriage to Crane didn't seem to be the all-embracing romantic love affair she might have wished. And certainly this could have been a perfect out for her. On the other hand, it is quite possible that she still loved Stephen. Or at least wanted to. The fine line between being in love with love and learning to really love somebody is difficult for some people to define. They will desperately cling to the dream.

When the child was born, there was some question as to whether either mother or child would survive. To complicate matters, Cheryl's blood contained an Rh-negative factor and it was necessary to give her transfusions in order to replace this with healthy blood.

Strangely enough, having a child made Lana feel, for the first time, that she was like any other woman. This was a feeling that she had been lacking from that day when her father had been killed.

Lana admitted to praying, with all her heart, for the survival of her little girl. Her prayers were, of course, answered, and the infant survived.

From the beginning, Cheryl was a sick and weak child.

The next year was filled with the joy of raising a baby, but also plagued with marital problems, which culminated in termination when Cheryl was one year old. Realizing the hopelessness of remaining together, the Cranes were divorced, but in the years that followed, they remained friends.

Lana resumed her habits of running wild, falling in and out of love and rushing into affairs. Lana found it impossible to control the irresistible impulse to seek lovers, regardless of the fact that she had a young daughter.

Some people have coldly pointed out that a divorcee with a child should force herself to live a "respectable" life and should devote her full attention to raising her child. A mother, however, still has physical needs. And some women simply will not find it possible to give up their lives to child-raising. Probably, under normal circumstances, it is smart to create a realistic balance that embraces both parenthood *and* a personal life. Including a career. Being a parent is an important part of a person's life, but certainly not the only a part of our living experience. A well-balance life involves many elements. Ignoring one for another can be dangerously destructive. A mother is more than just a parent, more than just a lover, and more than just a career. Ideally, it requires the blending of all elements that can bring success and happiness. Anything short of that would create different demands and limitations in our lives. This balancing act can be very difficult for any parent. The amazing thing is that anyone really comes out of it all in one piece. But we all do, to some degree or another.

It is when a person finds it difficult to truly define these basic areas of life, as they come in conflict with one another, that problems quickly follow.

For Lana Turner the elements were, of course, parent, career and love. And not necessarily in that order.

Lana seems to have never fully understood the true meaning of love, and admitted this when she said:

"The physical attracts me first. Then, if you get to know the man's mind and soul and heart, that's icing on the cake."

To some extent, this is true of everybody but Lana had never learned the difference between physical love and emotional love. She was spoiled by a career that made her, almost literally, a human goddess and there was money enough to buy anything her heart desired. What her body desired, she took. And apparently, if one is to believe the rumor mills, this involved sex with both men and women.

It has also been said of Lana that she was a very changeable woman, who emotionally didn't know in what direction she really wanted to go. Surely, she reacted to almost everything in a basically emotional way. Rather than thinking things out before acting, she let her heart rule her head.

She pointed this out herself when she said:

Whenever I do something, it seems so right. And turns out so wrong." Lana was referring directly to her experience in the world of living and loving.

Lana asked Louella Parsons, once: *"How does it happen that something that makes so much sense in the moonlight doesn't make any sense at all in the sunlight?"*

Maybe, in a way, she had always been a patsy for a man on the make—and there were numerous men flocking around her from whom she could take her pick.

One gets the picture of a woman who just had to look at a man to feel warm all over, the kind of woman who is basically sensual and unable to control the desires of the flesh. Spoiled by the Hollywood world she lived in, it is no wonder that she couldn't, as the song goes, "say no."

It wasn't too long before she became seriously interested in another man. This time it was Tyrone Power. They were seen together all the time and everybody thought this handsome couple would soon be walking down the aisle. Tyrone could have been a good father to Cheryl, and apparently Lana was well aware of this.

Then suddenly everything came to a jarring stop. The last time they were seen together was during a farewell party for Tyrone, who had been signed up to do a film in Rome. The party was an ideal occasion for an engagement announcement, and everybody present was expecting that. Lana and Tyrone were obviously very much in love. As it turned out, the party became a real farewell for Tyrone and Lana.

When in Rome, Tyrone met and dated a woman who would stop at nothing to get what she wanted, and she wanted Ty Power as her husband. Lana felt that the woman had turned Ty against her by telling him lies—though she never had proof. Nonetheless, Linda Christian became Power's bride and Lana was left out in the cold.

In time, Lana managed to get over the shock of losing Tyrone, and was seen in the company of the rich playboy Henry J. Topping. "Bob" Topping was a complete turnabout for Lana, since the only thing they seemed to have in common was their mutual reputation for romantic adventuring and patterns of marriage-divorce.

He became husband number three, and their marriage lasted long enough for Lana to have two miscarriages caused by the Rh-negative factor in her blood.

During that marriage they had some stormy times. One young lady circulated the following story about a night at the Turner/Topping home. She had been out with her date, apparently enjoying a very swinging intimate evening, and then they went to the Topping's home for what was supposed to be a "dinner" party. "Dinner" was served in cocktail glasses and consisted of nothing other than the cherries in Manhattans. The Toppings were dressed for a casual evening and it was just that, with a twist. Most people would consider their idea of a casual home party a bit far out. Drink followed drink until the hostess felt it was time to see a few movies.

According to the female guest's report, her first reaction was disappointment, since it didn't seem the kind of party that called for a Hollywood top feature. But the Toppings had their own special brand of motion pictures. According to the best of authority the picture viewed was titled *The Book Salesman* and depicted the failure of the salesman to sell books but his success in selling himself to the female "customers." Any young man thinking about selling books from door-to-door, who might have seen this picture, would get the idea that *not* making a sale to young females would be far more exciting and personally rewarding than making one. These were called stag-films. To-day they would be considered fairly mild stuff at the local video store adult department.

Pornography in films has been a popular source of income for people willing to do anything for money, because there is a large audience which delights in viewing the on-screen antics of two people intimately involved with each other. Errol Flynn was known to have a bedroom with a view-from-the-top, which made it possible to see the real-life action of two participants who would rather have had their activities in private.

The Book Salesman turned out to be a prime example of how far pornographic films will go. After the viewing it was suggested that a swim might be in order. The Topping's idea of an evening swim was to have plenty to drink and nothing to wear.

Lana supposedly pulled her husband into the pool. By that time it was early morning and enough liquor had been consumed to make everybody pretty fuzzy around the edges. Under such conditions, considering the evening's build-up, it's not too hard to imagine what was supposed to have gone on in the pool between husband and wife. But, it was reported, Lana, after a short time, stormed out of the pool, furious because her husband apparently offered the required action such a party seemed to demand.

Not very long after that the Toppings' marriage came to an abrupt end, but not before another little incident took place. It was one of those events that helped to strain the marriage bonds.

One night the Toppings' were "out on the town" with a couple of out-of-town guests and they ended up at *The Mocambo,* a nightclub once located on the Sunset Strip. Billy

Daniels, the famous black entertainer, was the star of the show and directed a goodly number of his songs toward Lana Turner, an item that wasn't ignored by the actress. After the last show, Daniels was asked to join the Topping party, where all sat talking and drinking until late in the morning, long after the club was officially closed. Finally Bob Topping suggested that they all go to their Holmby Hills home and continue the conversation in front of a cozy fireplace. So Daniels and his accompanist, Benny Payne—who had joined them some time earlier—left with the Topping party and they made their way to the more private setting of the host's home.

Those who saw, claimed drink followed drink and Billy went out of his way to please Lana, singing for her and to her. Obviously she enjoyed this to the fullest. Bob Topping suddenly decided he'd had enough and excused himself for the night. His friend had to help Bob get up to bed because the liquor had taken its effect.

For awhile things continued as before, with Billy giving out with the songs, Lana taking them in with every breath, and the drinks continuing to keep everybody in a fairly good mood. Then suddenly Billy Daniels must have thought it was time to sing a few quiet, personal songs to Lana, for the two of them disappeared into the den, leaving the rest of the guests to enjoy themselves.

At first things seemed to be going pretty well in the den with Lana and Billy, but suddenly a series of screams shattered the long silence and everybody rushed in to see what had happened. Though unable to go up to bed by himself, Bob Topping had found it easy enough to return silently, in pajamas, and interrupt what was going on between his wife and Daniels. What those present witnessed was an explosion of husbandry temper. Lana took a hard blow on the chin, which was powerful enough to shove her across the room and onto the couch. Name-calling by Bob Topping followed. No sooner had Lana recovered sufficiently to stagger to her feet than her husband was after her to deal out a repeat performance. At this point Daniels stepped in, trying to calm the enraged man. Daniels said something to the effect that Bob was drunk and should quit before things got out of hand—that he didn't know what he was doing. Topping turned on the singer, ordering him out of the house. Then he told his wife that he would deal with her later. With that parting shot at Lana he made a drunken swing at Daniels, which didn't connect. Bob's friend from out-of-town grabbed Bob and held him while Benny Payne, Daniel's accompanist, managed to get his boss out of the house before conditions became worse.

But it took more than Lana's bedroom tricks to ruin the marriage. Possibly what turned her sour enough on her husband to indulge in such escapades was the fact that her daughter, Cheryl, had been putting in a few words of her own about Topping. She claimed that his seemingly innocent business trips weren't all *that* innocent. Cheryl had the ability to disrupt her mother's marital happiness more than once. She was blamed for being directly responsible for breaking up three of Lana's marriages. Possibly it was a case of jealousy. Possibly Cheryl felt that her mother was away too much on motion picture locations and she didn't want to share any of her mother's time with strange men. Perhaps she resented the fact that Lana was always preoccupied with the opposite sex. Maybe she was merely a spoiled child who wanted things run her own way. There is good reason to believe that Cheryl considered Lana's men as competition for her affection.

But there was far more to all this than any of the above suggestions.

There is no question that Lana's wild four-and-a-half year marriage to Bob Topping came to an end partly as a result of her daughter's efforts to turn Lana against Bob—possibly in the mere childish attempt to gain attention.

During her marriage to Bob Topping, Lana had retired from pictures but as soon as divorce ended their relationship she returned to the Hollywood limelight. In 1951, while making *The Merry Widow,* she was romantically linked with her costar Fernando Lamas. Love scenes on the set were supposed to have been merely warm-ups for what went on later when they were alone. And Lana was still technically married to Topping while these stories about her and Lamas were circulating.

Cheryl was growing rapidly and was now an emotionally confused, gangling girl, hiding deep within herself. She was certainly aware of her mother's affairs and complications with men, though far too young to really understand their full meaning.

When Lana started dating Lex Barker it became quite clear, even to Cheryl's young mind, that the two were intimate and together. When Lana was in Europe with Lex, Cheryl joined her mother, but was soon sent away so that the movie Tarzan and Lana would have complete privacy.

Lex Barker was beginning to feel himself trapped in the Edgar Rice Burroughs' *Tarzan* role. It was suggested that he originally became interested in Lana because of the chance it offered to further his career. It can also be suggested that while they were married he took their vows seriously. Well, in a perverse sort of way, he was then clawing tooth and nail through the Hollywood jungle in an attempt to prove himself as an actor and get out of the *Tarzan* pictures. But, basically, Lex was a muscle-man who had been picked to play *Tarzan* as a replacement for the aging Johnny Weismuller—who had, until then, the exclusive right to the Tarzan role for many years because of a personal arrangement with the author and creator, Edgar Rice Burroughs. Whatever Lex might have thought of himself as an actor, it certainly wasn't what Hollywood power brokers had in mind.

Lana had always had a weakness for athletic men, and Lex Barker's physical proportions were outstanding. They were married in 1955, and from then on were thought by many Hollywood people as "queen" and "consort." Lana was the Super Star; Lex was nothing more than a tree-swinging ape-man. What an ego-bust for the muscle man!

Lana and Lex lived in the twenty-four-room villa and she was on one of her spending sprees. She had already made a fortune on her own and then married into another when she became Mrs. Bob Topping. It was even felt that Lana, afraid of another marital failure didn't see any reason to be thrifty. California divorce law splits community property down the middle!

Lex tried to convince Lana that she was spending far more than necessary. He was the type of man who believed in a tight budget. He suggested she set some kind of limit on how much money she spent on personal effects such as clothing and unnecessary luxuries. His advice seemed reasonable enough to

Lana, but in practice she found it hard to live under such financial limitations. One time after a shopping spree she announced that she'd bought a dozen pairs of shoes to match the dozen "gorgeous" gowns she'd purchased at *Don Loper's*. Lex, who was stunned by this announcement, especially after Lana's promise to cut down on spending, pointed out that her $1,500 monthly budget was already almost used up by this little escapade and only a week of the month had passed.

Lana is said to have answered: *"Don't worry about a thing, darling, I didn't spend a cent—in cash. I charged it!"*

In desperation, Lex consulted one of the many business managers of Hollywood who make a living by taking control of rich people's money, which they then invest in safe and profitable business ventures. The system works quite simply, and in almost every case is profitable to all concerned. The clients send all their income checks to the business manager who makes out a joint checking account, where both manager and client have to co-sign every check. The manager pays all the client's bills and sends along a weekly check, which might range from $50-200 for pocket money. For anyone unable to hold onto his money the minimum charge of 10% is repaid a hundredfold in tax advice and profits made on investments.

Lana agreed to consider the idea of a personal manager but when asked how much money she would require for each week, Lana announced that it might just be possible to get along with as little as $500. The business manager could hardly believe his ears. He was reported to have said to Lex: *"That woman doesn't need a manager; she should have a keeper."*

In 1956 Lana was again pregnant, but once more lost the baby. During this time Cheryl was attending a convent school because Lana felt that her daughter needed firm discipline and control. But Cheryl had other ideas and ran away from the school.

Cheryl's knowledge of her mother's private life made her feel she had no one to turn to for personal guidance. Even her father, Stephen Crane, wasn't in a position to exert any lasting influence. The experiences of her childhood were beginning to have their effect as she matured.

Lana, because of her own tragic childhood and lack of maturity, was in no position to act as counselor to her daughter.

The absence of a steadying masculine influence in the home during Cheryl's formative years left her insecure and confused so that she could not evaluate men properly.

Cheryl, therefore, could only judge men by those standards that were set up by daily experience. Men had come and gone in Lana's life, and for none did she reveal any lasting respect. Her attitude indicated complete lack of respect for all men. Lana, by example, had unwittingly indicated that sex was a plaything and that men were not trustworthy. This background was to be the important motive for Cheryl's later actions and relationships.

It was reported that Lex Barker sexually abused Cheryl —molesting her for a couple of years. When Lana learned of it—that was the end of their marriage. She kicked him out.

Lana, at the age of thirty-six, after twenty years being a star, found herself without a man. After her divorce from Lex Barker she and Cheryl lived a quiet and secluded life—at first. Lana honestly attempted to become the kind of mother her daughter needed, and for a time they developed a fairly close relationship. Possibly Lana felt that her failures in marriage and with her daughter were connected, and that it was time to solve the problem in a man-less environment.

But it couldn't last long, because Lana wasn't the kind of woman who could live a secluded life. During all the years since she'd been discovered in Schwab's, she'd enjoyed the constant admiration of all attractive Hollywood men, including many of the top male stars of the time.

A man who had little to do with the motion picture business, but lived, to some extent, on the borderline of Hollywood society now entered Lana's life. He had come from Chicago and years before had been a marine. He was, like all of Lana's lovers, handsome and muscular. His name was Johnny Stompanato, and he lived in the shadow of the underworld, a connection, which developed a feeling of terror in Lana as time went on.

Their relationship was far from the ideal, synthetic romantic interludes that marked Lana Turner's other affairs.

Johnny felt that when a woman got out-of-hand there was only one way to treat her—and he had enough muscle to make his theory a practical one.

It would be unfair to say that things weren't pleasant enough in the beginning. But as time went along, and Johnny used a little muscle to keep Lana in line, she found herself wanting to end the relationship, but didn't dare suggest such an idea.

Yet in 1957 things were still going along fairly smoothly. When Lana was in London with Cheryl, she wrote a letter to Johnny inviting him to join them during the Christmas Holidays—all expenses paid. There could be little question in Cheryl's mind as to what was going on between the adults. It has even been suggested that Cheryl herself had some romantic ideas about Johnny.

Things started getting rough when Johnny asked for a $10,000 loan, and a month later demanded $50,000. When Lana insisted she didn't have that kind of money he became furious and attempted to beat it out of her. Nonetheless, Lana still couldn't control her physical desire for this man.

On the night of April 4, 1958, in Hollywood at the Turner home, Johnny Stompanato lost his life. He was found with a knife wound in the abdomen. The newspapers were confused in their reports about the event. Some thought that Lana had found Johnny and Cheryl in bed together and being enraged, had killed her lover. Others thought that Cheryl seeing her mother manhandled by the man, ran to Lana's defense—with a knife. Another theory was that jealousy between the two women had caused the murder to take place. But out of the wild theories and contradictions emerged one final publicized pattern. *Cheryl was directly responsible for the murder of Johnny Stompanato, and had driven the knife into his stomach—either in a fit of jealous rage or in an attempt to save her mother's life, or, even, possibly by accident.*

The trial was a Roman holiday for the public. Lana had retained the famous Hollywood trial lawyer, Jerry Geisler, to defend her daughter against the State's charge.

As it turned out no criminal charges were brought against Cheryl, since the evidence seemed to indicate a sound, though possibly questionable motive, in that Cheryl was actually defending her mother. Only the two women really knew what happened and both gave identical evidence. The Court ruled, however, that Cheryl was to be first placed in the *El Retiro Home for Girls.* This was probably one of the worst mistakes possible. According to the best of evidence this is what happened:

Cheryl was ripe for what she found in the El Retiro Home: her entire background had prepared her for this event. She was prepared for this final lesson about life. She had already developed a dislike for men. Her experience with Lex Barker had been highly destructive. It was because of another man that she was now in the girls' detention home, legally separated from the mother who had helped to lead her to this final destiny. She was young, in her early teens. She was ready for the seclusion of an all-girl environment. Just when her sexuality was beginning to fully pop into being.

When teenagers are placed in confinement with members of their own sex, without any normal outlet for their newly-discovered sexual drives, they will find the only solution open to them—homosexuality.

Plus rape by a male close to them will create a very understandable hatred for men, and turn many women towards lesbianism.

According to medical records a brief period of homosexuality during puberty is not unknown, and for many, a normal part of growing up. Generally it doesn't have any damaging effects, providing the teenager soon recognizes the opposite sex as more desirable. It is a matter of early experimentation previous to seeking out heterosexual relations. We all go through a period of horror of the opposite sex right when our sexuality is developing. Most of us manage to avoid the confusion of homosexual experiences. Those that don't, sometimes get stuck in it, unable to escape. (Though, as modern research has revealed, true homosexuality is not conditioned by living experiences but often stems from a matter of biological factors. In other words: *not* a choice!)

Distort this natural instinct by segregating the sexes at the very point in their development when they might be dating normally, and there can be no question about the temptations that are offered.

It is a well-known fact that men at war, confined convicts, *and* boys and girls schools, are a perfect setting for homosexual practices. Where there is no other outset for sexual drives then many tend to use what is there.

This is a common reality. And most people return to their previously heterosexual preference. But some become defined by such experiences. Some scientific evidence now supports the belief that homosexuality for many may not be a choice.

Cheryl, during her stay in the *El Retiro Home for Girls,* learned the practice of Lesbianism. Supposedly it was a Mexican girl, one of her companions in the home, and "boss-girl," who was responsible for pushing Cheryl over the line. We will call her Nita. Nita at seventeen was the institution bully and a heavy drinker who had acquired an unhealthy liking for girls.

After a series of attempts to escape the *El Retiro Home,* over a period of eleven months, Cheryl was released into the care of her grandmother. Everything seemed to be going fairly well until Nita, released by El Retiro, suddenly turned up, and Cheryl became involved, once again with her girl friend. The situation came to a head when a party attracted the attention of neighbors to the Turner home, where Cheryl had been living with her grandmother. Since the elderly woman was known to be away, neighbors called the police.

While Cheryl later claimed it was nothing more than a teenagers' pajama party, the police had good reason to believe differently when they broke into the house. They discovered a drunken brawl in progress with a "crew cut" Nita dressed like a man, calling the turns for Cheryl and another young female guest.

The fact that Lana was filming a multi-million dollar movie at the time made it necessary for studio executives to do everything within their power to keep the scandal unpublicized.

The police didn't press their case very hard at this point because of the studio involvement and the fact that she was Lana's daughter. But it became obvious that something had to be done when Cheryl disappeared, leaving a note behind which explained that she had to get away to think things out.

Lana, herself, during this period, had married a man named Fred May. After Cheryl returned home the difficulties, which she was causing became so intensified that it was necessary for the Mays to appear in court. Cheryl and Stephen Crane also were in court. Apparently Cheryl managed to convince the Judge that there was at least some reasonable doubt as to the actual events during her party with Nita. No action was taken against Cheryl, but Judge Harry Simon announced that it would be better for the girl if she were sent to what was politely referred to as a "special boarding school." Cheryl was sent to a Connecticut Institute where "emotionally unbalanced" wealthy people were sent. Here, every effort was made to help Cheryl develop an understanding of herself and life and about her place in the sexual and social world. Apparently a change was effected in Cheryl's outlook on life. Upon returning to Hollywood, she announced her desire to live on her own, and stand on her own two feet.

Lana's career picked up during this period. She had now made two successful films, *Imitation of Life* and *By Love Possessed.*

Louella Parsons, in her book, *Tell It to Louella* expressed the opinion of others who had watched the racy and wild career of Lana Turner: that Lana had finally changed and matured.

When Lana married Fred May she said:

"Love—the real thing—isn't a wild passion. It's based on companionship and respect; on mutual interests and an admiration for the man in your life."

There was little question in anybody's mind that Lana had married Fred May, already a father who loved children, because she truly believed he would be a good influence on her daughter. Yet the events which led to Cheryl's commitment to the Connecticut "boarding school" took place after this fruitless marital attempt of Lana's.

Lana Turned *had* changed, had matured, had developed more realistic and adult attitudes toward life and love, placing sex and intimacies with men in their proper perspective. She *had* assumed the full responsibilities of motherhood, doing everything possible to help her daughter.

Even then things were not perfect.

Tragically, Cheryl's experiences, particularly in corrective homes, left too deep an impression on her mind to be wiped out.

Lana began to feel that all efforts to get closer to her daughter or to change her way of life were hopeless.

Then Cheryl rented an apartment with another girl, who we will call Sally, and started modeling lingerie. When Fred May discovered this he tried to persuade Lana to discourage her, but the actress merely said, "Let Cheryl do what she wants, if it makes her happy."

The modeling continued and then developed into something far more startling when Cheryl, Bobbie Gentry and Diane Lewis teamed together for an act at a third-rate Sunset Strip night club, the *Summit.* When Cheryl did her disrobing act there wasn't much question about the look in her roommate's eyes as she watched. Sally made no attempt to hide the deep personal attachment she felt toward Cheryl.

The fact that Cheryl Crane was over eighteen and legally allowed, in California, to decide her future, made it impossible for Lana to control her daughter's life any longer. What might go on in that apartment with Sally would be hard to prove one way or another unless there were eyewitnesses, but there seemed to be little reason to believe that Cheryl had forgotten what she learned in the *El Retiro Home.*

As for Lana's marriage to Fred May, it too, could not last long. Frustrated by Lana's conviction that there wasn't anything to be done for Cheryl, the first seeds of divorce sprouted. When Cheryl suggested that Fred was actually more interested in her than appeared on the surface, Lana Turner reacted as she had always done in the past when her daughter implied that a husband was showing undue attention and affection toward his stepdaughter.

Lana Turner's lifelong fight with her daughter never ended. It had started at the very beginning when child-birth almost took the actress' life, when she herself was too immature to know the difference between sexual attraction and love. And the constant conflict had continued. She wandered from man to man in a desperate attempt to find the satisfaction that fame and fortune had never been able to give her. Her battle saw a temporary truce when Johnny Stompanato was stabbed to death and mother stood solidly behind daughter. And Lana, who had in the beginning looked for love in sex, found herself, once more alone, because of this mother-daughter conflict which had always managed to break all ties with her husbands and lovers. In the end, both suffered. Even under the best conditions, a daughter can turn wild and run down the hopeless path of personal and emotional self-destruction.

Now they are two women, as different from each other as night and day. Yet, in a strangely odd way, each was morally bankrupt. Each faced an uncertain future, one that was always blackened by scandal. Did Lana, in a fit of jealous rage, stab Johnny Stompanato? Or was it, in truth, the action of her frustrated, misguided teen-age daughter?

One thing is certain: a mother-daughter relationship is a delicate thing, and as with any relationship, it is mutual. Lana, the adult, must surely have felt that she had failed her daughter, and possibly it was true. On the other hand, might it be that each, in her own way—perhaps not to the same degree—failed the other.

Be that true or not. Lana died of throat cancer in 1995.

Hopefully, Cheryl has finally found inner peace, regardless of all those young childhood experiences living with the famous Lana Turner. One can only hope that Cheryl has come to terms with all those turbulent experiences and found happiness.

PART SIX

THE RISE AND FALL OF MARILYN MONROE

"I've always felt those articles somehow reveal more about the writers than they do about me."

The mystery of Marilyn Monroe's death will never be truly solved. Even in life her story was so confused and distorted by writers as to lend a veil forever over her legend. Much of the mystery was partly Marilyn's fault.

Louella Parsons felt that Marilyn had gotten to the point where she found it hard to tell the difference between fact and fantasy. It is almost understandable, considering the actress' early, lonely life, living in foster homes, where only through her active imagination that she was able to find any form of escape.

Another reason for the confusion surrounding Marilyn Monroe is suggested in her own comment about the authors who wrote about her.

Nonetheless, it is a fact that in the twelve years Marilyn worked in films she appeared in twenty-four motion pictures, which reportedly made $200,000,000 at the box office. She was the sex symbol of the American public and was loved by the entire world, yet considering her own personal life, this was a cruel irony, which helped push her towards the edge of self-destruction.

From the promotions liberally handed out, and the image she projected on the screen, and for the public, Marilyn was a shallow sex-pot, unable to understand her full effect on the male animal. Yet nothing could have been further from the truth.

Such statements as the following were generously attributed to her image, helping to project this false impression.

"I like to feel blonde all over."

"When I sleep, I wear Chanel No. 5."

Attractive, sensual statements to intrigue and delight a male audience which adored her.

Marilyn, in her private life, was completely unpredictable, and seldom did anybody know exactly what to expect from her.

Hedda Hopper tells the story of when Marilyn arrived for an interview, wearing a beige fur collar on a beige coat, and a beige dress to match her beige hair. Hopper asked: "Are you beige all over?" And Marilyn, without thinking, started to lift her dress, and then embarrassed, exclaimed, "Oh, Hedda, that's *vulgar.*"

Many reports about Marilyn Monroe would suggest a far more sexually liberated woman who had, perhaps, slept her way to fame, using the "Hollywood Casting Couch" as a road to the top. Other reports suggest she simply had a lot of lovers. Some claimed she was over-sexed; others suggested she was really sexually frigid. The conflicting list of rumors and gossip was endless and continually fed on it until it really became quite difficult to be certain what might be the truth.

Over the years she was connected to a number of famous celebrities and power brokers. Supposedly her list of lovers included an amazing array of "playboys" including some in Washington, D.C.

Truth or legend is at times difficult to separate.

They say a beautiful woman can get away with a lot and Marilyn certainly did everything in her power to prove that. There was little doubt about her attractiveness to the male sex, with measurements of 37-23-37, and a personal magnetism, which could project itself not only on the screen but in person as well. Even those she worked with who were often pushed beyond their ability to control their tempers, felt the impact of her charm.

160

She was notorious for her chronic negligence to appear on the set on time Her tardiness irritated more than one producer and director. She was quoted as saying, *"It's not really me that's late; it's the others who are always in such a hurry."*

Yet she admitted in a more sober and honest mood,

> When I have to be somewhere for dinner at 8 o'clock, I'll lie in the bathtub for an hour or longer. Eight o'clock will come and go and I still remain in the tub. I keep pouring perfumes into the water and letting the water run out and filling the tub with fresh water. I forget about 8 o'clock and my dinner date. I keep thinking and feeling far away.
>
> Sometimes I know the truth of what I'm doing. It isn't Marilyn Monroe in the bath but Norma Jean (her real name). I'm giving Norma Jean a treat. She used to have to bathe in water used by six or eight other people. Now she can bathe in water as clean and transparent as a pane of glass.

With all her apparent "innocence," Marilyn was a highly temperamental woman who could be extremely irritating to those who worked with her.

> When I finally start putting my clothes on I move as slowly as I can. I begin to feel a little guilty because there seems to be an impulse in me to be as late as possible. It makes something in me happy—to be late. People are waiting for me. People are eager to see me. I feel a queer satisfaction punishing the people who are wanting me now. But it's not them I'm really punishing. It's the long-ago people who didn't want Norma Jean.

And another time she said: *"I don't know why people are so upset about my being late. Frankly, I'm surprised I get anywhere at all."*

Such were some of the contrasts of Marilyn Monroe, and even in her own words she argued with herself.

Yet she wasn't the only one who dealt with lack of consideration, for she was also victimized, not only in her youth but also in her career. And as some have said, even in her death.

The following annotate about her may have been some publicity story "invented" by a skilled writer. It was certainly cute and with a biting sense of humor. It sounds like a very intelligent woman playing a very smart game. It has the ring of truth and I like to think it was actually said by Marilyn.

When she was making *Gentlemen Prefer Blondes,* the studio paid her a mere $500 a week, while Jane Russell was demanding and getting $200,000, plus extras. She didn't even have a private dressing room. Marilyn later said that she complained to her bosses, saying: *"Look! After all, I am the blonde and it is "Gentlemen Prefer Blondes." But still they always kept saying 'Remember, you're not a star.' And I said, "Well, whatever I am, I am the blonde!"*

And not the dumb blonde the studio people would have liked to believe.

This kind of irritation continued on and off throughout her career, even to *Something's Got to Give,* for which Fox was going to pay her a mere $100,000, to Dean Martin's $300,000. Her career between those two pictures was a stormy one, personally and professionally.

She attempted semi-retirement from public life when she married Arthur Miller, and for almost three years she didn't make any pictures. This cost her a great loss of popularity, and when returned to Hollywood to make *Some Like It Hot* there was some doubt as to whether she could make the comeback.

Some Like It Hot was one of Marilyn's biggest box office successes.

But during the time when she wasn't making films there had been some vital evidence as to her loss of popularity. Her fan mail, which had been 10,000 letters a week when she worked for Fox, dropped to an all-time low of fifty letters a week.

Marilyn fought hard to hang on to her career during the last part of her life. It had become her life, but even more importantly, a major motive for living. In her last months, Marilyn had little else but her career, which she feared didn't have very much longer to go. She had been disappointed in her personal life, in her inability to have children. She had fears about losing her beauty. She was always proud of her body, and enjoyed spending hours looking at herself in a mirror, admiring the lovely, full, supple curves which had helped to make her famous.

This inner insecurity showed itself in many ways. Her driving need for perfection haunted her life. Even when others were satisfied with one of her performances she would insist on doing it over again until every action was perfect, every movement of her eyes and hands seemed just right. And even then she would turn to her husband, or personal acting coach, for approval. She demanded the right to okay every photograph before release, going over them again and again, vetoing any one that gave her the slightest cause for hesitation.

Her doubts were complicated by the fact that she allowed so many people to give her advice, which she regretfully took too seriously. She searched, throughout her life for truth, for happiness, some place which would finally give her a sense of security but she never seemed to find it long enough to create a lasting impression.

This inability to find happiness, this inner fear and sense of insecurity had its physical manifestations. She was highly nervous and sensitive to what went on around her, to what people did and said; so much so that she made enemies of people who actually meant no harm. Colleagues were many times, merely kidding, or being playful with her. On the set of *Some Like It Hot* she reached a high point of irritating those around her. This self-doubt and super-sensitivity many times affected her professionally to the point where she would fluff her lines over and over again in simple scenes where there should not have been any difficulty whatsoever.

Her insecurity reached the point of ridiculousness while she was making the picture *Bus Stop*: she walked off the set because Hope Lange had blonde hair. She had gone to Joshua Logan, who was responsible for the picture and demanded that Miss Lange darken her hair. When Logan refused, she refused to work until she got her way. Her insecurity was threatened by the fact that Hope Lange had blonde hair. Nobody other than herself could have considered such a possibility. Not only were they two different types of actresses, but Marilyn Monroe should have known that her own ability, her own personal magnetism, would not be in danger from anyone other than herself.

Hedda Hopper has said, *"There is no such thing as a happy artist. They develop an understanding about things that other people don't understand."*

The very things, which make an artist frustrated, are many times those elements that make them great artists. Their sensitivity, their ability to see their own faults and the wrongs of the world about them, help to make them all the more understanding of the parts they are playing, able to go into the minds of fictional characters and bring them to life.

They escape into these fantasies, fictional people, in a desperate attempt to escape their own self-doubts. Shy people turned into make-believe creatures on stage or film. The actor many times is attracted to the profession especially because of this very element: becoming other people than themselves— even if for just a short time. They have stood on stage or before a camera doing things that in real life would be totally impossible for them to even consider.

Marilyn was basically, in the beginning, an unsophisticated woman who got caught up in a world of fame, a world which gave her all the material things a person might want, yet made her pay the price in the lack of privacy. She enjoyed being loved by the public, yet, at the same time, desired the same simple things that all women want: love, family, children, and a sense of security.

From the very beginning, Marilyn's personal life was tragic. She was, in a way, the Cinderella of the 1900s, who came not only from the loneliness of foster homes, but was the illegitimate daughter of a woman who wasn't emotionally able to raise her.

She never knew her father, and throughout her life she was always seeking a substitute for that missing parent. All her husbands were some years older.

Jim Daugherty was six years older than Marilyn. Joe DiMaggio's span was twelve years. Miller was Marilyn's senior by eleven years.

Marilyn claimed that she thought sex was important, but never actually married for it. She claimed to have married for love and happiness—except for a first marriage, which was a desperate attempt to escape the foster homes.

Even though she claimed to think often of sex, and was one of the biggest sex symbols in the '50s, there are some that doubt she actually enjoyed it.

Marilyn claimed, *"Sex is important to me. I think one of the reasons everyone thinks me so sexy is that I think about sex all the time. I wonder about sex with every man I meet, and they sense it and—well, respond."*

But John Huston stated: *"Within the international sex symbol that is Marilyn Monroe, is a nice, quiet young woman fighting to get out. In fact I don't think she really cares very much about sex at all."*

There were, as Huston stated, good reasons to believe that Marilyn Monroe had never really found true satisfaction with any man. She was like the true nymphomaniac (who is the female counterpart to the Don Juan) who though seemingly unable to get enough lovers, actually can never experience orgasm during congress with a male partner. The true nympho will frantically seek out every male partner she is able to seduce in a desperate search to discover that one particular man who can prove that she is like any other woman. The true nymphomaniac, according to all medical authorities, is a very sick and tragic woman, who should be locked up, away from the public, where she can do no harm to herself or to others. This kind of woman is much like the playboy who is out to seduce every female he can. Between two normal people, in love, the idea of seeking out another partner for sexual acts is not so much repulsive as undesirable. Insofar as they have a healthy response to the opposite sex, they rather seek something that they find undesirable, because it cannot ever be as fully meaningful as with the person they love. To a healthy couple, sex without love is as hopeless as love without sex.

And Marilyn Monroe had many things working against her finding an ideal relationship with men: a childhood rape, the foster homes which had little love for this young girl who had been thrust upon them. At one time she lived with a family of religious fanatics who taught her that sex, drinking and smoking were un-Godly sins. Under such influences, it is not surprising that Marilyn would find it difficult to have a normal attitude toward sex and love.

Some might wonder why she would run from man to man. Yet it is a psychological truth that many times people will react completely opposite to what their personal convictions might dictate. It is surely difficult to accept the fact that the public sex symbol couldn't experience personal and satisfactory relationships with men. Perhaps that was simply part of the myth. One would like to believe this, but the evidence does somewhat lean in the opposite direction, revealing a tortured life, plagued by personal doubts, fears, and guilt. We all have to struggle just to survive many terrible personal experiences. But it is difficult to believe that a woman who reached such international fame, gained such devout love from the world at large would not feel she had a wonderful life. Nothing could be further from the truth. She was a tormented woman from the very beginning, and that lasted throughout her life.

The personal and private living experience of each one of us is far more complicated. Seeming success in our careers does not automatically mean happiness in our private lives.

Messages taught in childhood can be damaging as well as helpful. When we are given the wrong message it can have damning effects in later life.

Guilt and fears can do horrid things to the human body and mind. Add the fact that Marilyn's whole childhood was lacking from any true example of real love, and it becomes un-derstandable that she became a confused and unhappy woman, failing in her marriages and love affairs. Her private life had become a shallow place, which gave her no real happiness.

Even with her worldwide fame she was unable to find security—and only experienced terrible doubts and fears that drove her into the nightmare lands of drugs. And in the end, even her career seemed to go on a downhill slide. Without love in childhood it can be difficult to really understand the full meaning of it in adulthood, for love is a full giving of oneself, an experience of selflessness. It is both an instinct and an art.

Marilyn's career was professionally an over all success, even though there were plenty of ups and downs even though she held tragic doubts about what she had managed to do in a fairly short time. She rose only to finally fall into a pit that ended in death.

At thirty-five her popularity among directors had hit a low. People who, years before would have been willing to do anything to sign her up for a picture couldn't care less during these later years. Not only had her reputation been marred by a long-standing habit of being late, independent and difficult to work with, but also many Hollywood people believed her figure was at last showing the signs of age. And she wasn't the young girl who had become so famous within a very few years anymore.

Yet even during this low ebb in her career, there still were people who clamored for the Monroe magic, willing to take chances with her. She was considering roles like the leads in *Breakfast At Tiffany's,* and *Paris Blues,* with Marlon Brando, and a television production of *Rain,* all of which fell through for one reason or another. The fact was that her career was failing. But even before the last low period, it never was quite right even in her own eyes. Perhaps these doubts were the normal ones that come to creative people—no matter how much success is behind you, it is necessary to top the last Big One! In their mind it is an endless climb upwards, always attempting to get better, and never quite convinced they ever were really very good. We all see ourselves from the inside with all the inner demons and doubts and imperfections stripped naked within our minds. We can't escape that. And the highly sensitive creative artist who is publicly worshipped as, in her case, a Goddess, it becomes even more difficult to live up to an image one knows is false. She was considered a sex symbol. She was the dream girl every man wanted to possess.

This public image did not match her personal self-image. To Marilyn it was impossible to live up to this myth.

Yet, it was this worshipping public who wanted her, loved her, that keep Marilyn going—and at the same time was a personal torment, for she felt it was impossible to live up to the image. Her reality was totally different from her public image—an image the world loved.

Of course it was the Goddess that was so adored. The Monroe of movie fame and fan magazines and media stories. The MM of the PR promos. This was not the real woman inside, the Norma Jean who still existed within her famous body.

Marilyn, a nervous, fair-skinned woman, started taking sleeping pills some ten years before her death. In the last years she was so addicted to barbiturates that it would have killed her to get off the pills.

Yet with all these frustrations, all these personal faults and failures, Marilyn, in the beginning and the end, adored her only lasting love affair, which had been with her fans all over the world. The public, even from the beginning, was her only true lover, her only Prince Charming.

She believed that she really belonged to the fickle and demanding public. And, in a way, what she couldn't find in private life, she received from the impersonal public, which was always at arms distance from the real Marilyn—the Norma Jean who wanted love and affection. Marilyn, herself, realized this. She once said:

> I guess I had known it all the time. I knew what I had known when I was 13 and walked along the sea edge in a bathing suit for the first time. I knew I belonged to the public and to the world, not because I was talented or even beautiful but because I had never belonged to anyone else. The public was the only family, the only Prince Charming, and the only home I had ever dreamed about.

To fully probe the mystery that was Marilyn and attempt to understand the far greater mystery of what truly took her life it is necessary to study the frustrations which plagued her every day. One needs to examine the struggles, which made the kind of woman who could sit in a lonely room, and either by design or accident take her life.

Her story starts on June 1, 1926, in a Los Angeles hospital. The name given on the birth certificate was Norma Jean Mortenson; the last name was changed to Baker by one of Marilyn's several foster parents some time later. Her father was a Danish immigrant named Edward Mortenson. There is little known about him, except that he allowed Norma Jean to be born illegitimately. Her mother was a stage struck woman who worked as a film cutter and Marilyn's early life revolved around movie fan magazines. The two of them lived with her mother's best friend, Grace McKee, who was, in a short time, to become the closest thing Marilyn would have to a true "mother". But at an early stage, the two basically simple women, both great fans of the movies, created for the young Norma Jean an atmosphere, which developed in the child an awareness of the glamour and excitement of the motion picture business.

Shortly after Norma Jean's birth her father died in a motorcycle accident, and her mother's influence was cut short by a nervous breakdown, which sent her to a sanitarium. It was this fact, in later years, and knowledge that her mother's parents had gone insane, that was one of the reasons for Marilyn's undercurrent of self-doubt and fear. She lived in constant horror that she herself would go insane.

Grace McKee for awhile kept Norma Jean under her protective wing and was actually made her legal guardian when her mother was labeled legally incompetent to raise the child. But Grace McKee finally found it too difficult to raise the child and work at the same time and was forced to turn her over to a foster home.

From then on Marilyn had a series of foster parents, spaced only by painful experiences in orphan homes. She reportedly had a dozen foster parents. This was hardly conducive of teaching a child about mother and father love. Or creating any sense of security within her. These tragic years were marked by two major shocking events. When she was two years old a deranged neighbor was reported to have attempted to kill her with a pillow. At six a family "friend", an event that left an obviously large scar on her life, raped her. Before that, at five, Norma lived with a family who treated her like the bad sisters in the Cinderella story, having her scrub floors and help with the family laundry. To make things worse, Norma Jean's experience with this family of religious fanatics impressed on the small child's impressionable mind that sex itself was dirty and sinful.

Norma Jean was twelve when she first started to blossom out into a young woman. Up to that point she'd been called, true to the nature of young children, "Norma Jean the Human Bean." But when she discovered that by wearing a sweater the boys' reactions were quite different, she began, for the first time in her life, to find a natural place for herself in the social life of the teen-age world. Her impact on the neighborhood created some rather nasty name-calling, but this apparently had little influence on her. She was finally getting the attention, which she craved and needed. Before this she had been lonely, unloved, in the way most of us would think of love. But now she was discovering that an attractive body got attention. Even then, like many teen-age girls, she went through a period of withdrawing. She dreamed of Clark Gable as an ideal father.

Marilyn told reporters about this phase in her life, while being interviewed at the Cedars of Lebanon Hospital in Los Angeles, apparently offering up a bit of her young dream-world:

> I was one of a family of many children, and Clark Gable was our father, and he liked me the best. Each night, when he came home, he'd swing me up onto his shoulder and tell me how pretty I was. Of all the children, he loved me the best.

By fourteen, Marilyn was fully matured, and also fully aware of the power of her body on the opposite sex. How thrilling and rewarding it must have been for a shy, insecure young girl.

170

She developed a healthy liking for boys, which was returned in full measure. Even at this age Marilyn was learning that she had a special place in the world of men. She learned to dress herself in tight, form-fitting sweaters and skirts, which accented every curve.

She now lived with her Aunt Grace, who had married a man named Goddard, of Van Nuys. Probably this was one of the happier times in her childhood, because of the attention her attractive figure was winning and because she was living with the woman she'd known from the very beginning of her life.

Teenage life can be difficult to everybody. But to discover you are a major attraction of the opposite sex has to have been wonderful.

It was while living here that Marilyn met Jim Daugherty, the son of neighbors who lived down the block from the Goddard's. When Mr. Goddard decided to move East, and didn't want to take Marilyn along, the only escape possible seemed marriage—to anyone. Both Jim's parents and the Goddards were in favor of marriage between the two young people. Marilyn was sixteen then, and even though too young to possibly have any idea of the true meaning of love, willingly fell into a marriage with a young boy for whom she felt no more than affection. Of course, at that age none of us truly know what end is up and think we're "in love" with the first person that attracts us. Hormones being what they are! Of course, nobody can truly know what is going on in another's mind. But even if she was "in love" it was apparently "puppy love"—and a means out of "parental" domination and a kind of "grown-up" freedom.

This marriage, Marilyn admitted years later, was an escape, an attempt to find some kind of personal security. This desperate attempt of an innocent, frustrated teen-ager, who had never really known what it was like to be fully loved—and had never been really able to think of any place she lived as home—turned into the first of many marital failures.

One story told about this marriage with Jim Daugherty is typical to some extent of many stories of newlyweds. Marilyn, knowing little about cooking, but determined not only to make a go at a marriage which was, unknown to her, doomed from the beginning, wanted to please her husband with something different for dinner. Somewhere she had read, or been told, that the Japanese considered raw fish a very popular delicacy. Jim worked in an aircraft factory, and was an uncomplicated young man, without the sophistication to understand or appreciate a young wife's attempts to please him. When she served the raw fish, he reacted automatically, making it obvious, in no uncertain terms, that he not only didn't find raw fish his kind of dish, but also resented it, in light of the nation's war with Japan. The explosion that followed caused the hurt and sensitive brides to take hold of a garbage can and hurl it at her ungrateful husband. Jim retaliated by grabbing his bride and pushing her into the shower, to cool her off with a cold bath. This did teach Norma Jean that she had a husband who could handle her with an iron hand, if necessary. And even though it seemed in theory to be—though not in practice—the discipline that she needed (and in life searched for), it was one example of the impossible difficulties that would, in the end, manage to break up their marriage.

Jim took pictures of Norma Jean, being rightfully proud of the young woman he had married, and the beautiful figure she possessed. Apparently he showed these to his fellow workers at the aircraft plant. As it can only happen in real life, Robert Mitchum, who also happened to be working at the factory, saw the pictures. Years later he would star with Marilyn Monroe in *River of No Return.*

Norma Jean and Jim managed to stay together for four years, but in 1947 it was obvious that they couldn't possibly continue such a failing marriage, and Marilyn got her divorce. Jim went into the Merchant Marine and out of her life forever, and Marilyn took the first steps that would finally make her an international star.

No doubt the reaction of her friends to Marilyn's pictures helped to influence her to consider modeling. She was working at an airplane factory when she started posing for cheesecake pictures.

It was an army photographer who was indirectly responsible for giving Marilyn her first start. He had been assigned to take pictures of the airplane *factory,* and happened to get a few shots of Norma Jean, which he later showed to Potter Hueth, a commercial photographer. Hueth was immediately interested and offered to take pictures of Norma Jean, it she would pose for him on spec.

Norma Jean showed, even then, an instinctive ability to be natural before the camera, to project the animal sex appeal, which was in time to become the polished image of Marilyn Monroe. Her trademark!

These pictures led to more, until Emaline Snively, who ran a school and agency for modeling, became interested in Norma Jean. Emaline, like Hueth, took a personal interest in Norma Jean and willingly helped her, without charge, until she had managed to get assignments. Norma Jean was to have many people like Emaline Snively enter her life and give the helping hand that would lead her to fame. She worked hard, and was on time for all appointments. Her sexuality and figure were obvious material for pinup pictures.

Any woman who has the attractiveness which Norma Jean possessed, and is willing to cooperate with others, will, in time, find the right people willing to help her along the way. Nobody is an island unto himself, and in show business, as in any other business, it's impossible to do it all by oneself. Through Emaline's efforts along with others around her, Norma Jean began to appear in magazines, and in poses designed to attract the male eye. Not such a difficult job to do effectively. She photographed beautifully and was a willing subject.

One pair of eyes her pictures attracted were those of the powerful Howard Hughes, who was famous for being able to pick female stars. Harlow and Russell were directly in his debt for their stardom. And Hughes became indirectly responsible for Norma Jean getting her first screen test, though at the time he probably wasn't even aware of it.

It was through the efforts of Ben Daniels, then working for 20th Century Fox Studios as one of its head talent scouts, that a screen test came Norma Jean's way. An agent, who announced that a Norma Jean Daugherty was attracting Hughes' attention, had called him. This agent declared that if Ben believed Fox might be interested, he had better work hard and fast. The agent gave him two days.

At the time Zanuck was head of Fox, and he was "King"! His word was law, his smallest desire was a command. Nobody did anything without Zanuck's okay. He held in his hands the control of some of Hollywood's most famous stars, and could make or break them like others might strike a match.

Ben attempted to get hold of Zanuck in time to beat the deadline, but Zanuck was unavailable. Ben had to decide if he could take the chance of going ahead with the test, alone, without Zanuck's okay. In the end he decided to do it on his own.

Ben Daniels made sure that very few people knew what was going on, doing everything in secret, with only those directly involved knowing anything about it.

Norma Jean was given a form-fitting, sequin-covered dress to wear, and told to walk across the set, putting as much sex into the walk as possible. The results are easily guessed. The test was everything that Ben would have wished. The impact of innocent sexiness fairly exploded on the screen. Ben's gamble had paid off in spades.

Zanuck was invited to see the film test and was so impressed that he forgot that it had been done without his consent. He insisted she be signed to a studio contract.

The first matter of business was to change Norma Jean's name. Ben suggested the name of Marilyn, mainly because Norma Jean reminded him of the one-time Broadway star Marilyn Miller. Monroe had been a family name of her mother's and was a natural match. And thus was born the name, if not, as yet, the star Marilyn Monroe.

But the years of struggle had just started. Nothing comes easy even for over-night discoveries. And, strangely enough, she wasn't even that!

The signing of a studio contract doesn't make a person a star any more than having a first drink makes a person an alcoholic. It takes time and effort, not only of the individual involved but also of many other people.

Darryl Zanuck was the "Star Maker" of Fox, and without his personal interest, and backing, a young talent could rot in place until the short-term contract had run out. Regardless of the fact that the name of Marilyn Monroe had been born, and she was standing at the doorway of fame, glamour and stardom, the door was still nicely closed. She was like a new born baby who had to learn, who had to go through the growing pains until full maturity could catch the attention of her elders. At this point she was simply another pretty baby face (and body) and little more. Talent and beauty in Hollywood is cheap, for starry-eyed young people are continually drawn to the city; everybody wants to become a movie star! Many find the casting couch their final destination, being used as toys for power brokers that have no consideration for the needs and feelings of these innocent, desperate young people. The film industry was no different than any other business—and a person with power will use it to get whatever it is they want. In fact, one of the most seductive elements of power is the use of it over others. These casting couchers used pretty young bodies like candy to be devoured and forgotten.

And Marilyn was one beautiful, lovely, desperately dedicated young lady, selling sex as her major product! One wonders just how far she had to play the game. The fact that she made it to the top, rather than being tossed brutally aside by the casting directors and talent scouts and agents and producers, writers, you name it, suggests she learned to play her hand in a smart way. And sleeping with every Tom, Harry and Dick who offered themselves as prizes to please in order to have doors open, wasn't very smart business. This is not to say she didn't know the game, nor that she may not have been used, or even used it, but certainly whatever she actually did to win her place in motion picture history was successful.

With her background it isn't difficult to imagine a woman who slept her way to fame, using her body to get ahead; and it is equally as easy to assume she had been very selective in how she used that power over men. One could even imagine her being able to invite passes while blocking them; one can even wish that perhaps she had played the vamp game without throwing herself into the arms of these studio executives. Sometimes it is possible to by-pass the bedroom demands of powerful men. Sometimes a smart person gets ahead on looks and talent, luck and connections without becoming a sexual toy.

Sometimes.

Only those who are involved know their parts on this side of Marilyn's climb to fame. Most are dead. What is left is the evidence of reporting at the times and some obvious events, which apparently did take place—and were never questioned.

Marilyn was no fool. She was an intelligent woman. Not a dumb blonde. She might have appeared innocent, and child-like, but hardly inexperienced. What she hadn't learned early in life she quickly learned later. What she needed to do in order to become successful as a Sex Queen, she did. And, of course, there where the lovers.

One would like to believe she was smart enough to pick her lovers, and that she had taken advantage of them, rather than the other way around. Probably it was somewhere in between. Nobody goes through life without being taken advantage of at one time or another. And nobody is successful on good looks, talent and luck. It takes the combination of many events, people, and lucky moments. Timing has a lot of influence. Accident. But most of all it is a matter of having the right product for sale at the moment when it is exactly what somebody is looking to buy. And it is necessary to have the public relations departments feeding out the right balance of material to sell a bright young product to a public. And the studios had some excellent PR departments. But even the public has to be ready for the particular product being sold.

Trouble is—one doesn't get to first base until the men in power offer up the "Go" command.

While Zanuck had liked the screen test, and had been impressed enough to have Marilyn signed up by the studio, he thought of her merely as starlet material. A starlet is nothing more than a young actress whose life has been taken over by the studio. For her weekly check she is supposed to do everything they tell her. They guide her professional and private life. She will be asked to appear in public as nothing more than attractive decoration, pose for publicity pictures, and help promote the studio's pictures.

In those days the studios still had their ranks of contract players who were nothing more than show pieces, beautiful bodies to fancy up any publicity campaign. Some people coldly think of starlets as nothing more than party girls. A cleaned up name for prostitutes. There are many who were willing to give all the young studio executives and big brass the freedom of their bodies, hoping they would attract the right kind of attention from the right kind of people. These became nothing more than toys for the casting couchers. Few made it beyond the couch, most were passed from one office to another, then tossed out onto the "streets of Hollywood" when their contracts ground to an end. Some end up as prostitutes or simply get married, most passed into the background, merging with the thousands of other wanna-bee failures. And these were the ones who came "so close" to making it big.

They had "almost" made it! So the legend goes. They'd come close.

They'd had a short-term studio contract. Very few got past that first contract. But not all were turned into sexual toys. Many were simply not willing to play that game. And while very few made it to the top; most failed.

None made it very far without the right connections.

And there is a great difference between being a couch toy to be tossed aside or cheaply shared and carefully connecting with the right people and allowing intimacy to follow in a natural, smart way. Having an affair can be far different from playing the quickie party-girl game.

It has been claimed that Marilyn Monroe didn't use her body in this way, even though she admittedly had her affairs. In view of the fact that in time she did make her mark on the Hollywood scene, it would seem that her claim is, at least in the most part, true. For most of those women willing to sell their bodies for movie roles ended up as casualties tossed onto the sidelines.

It takes talent, guts and the ability to know who to sleep with, and who *not* to sleep with. And luck. And timing. And an endless chain of events, which drives one down the road to fame and success.

And in many cases they end in great personal tragedy.

There is much evidence that Marilyn Monroe became a star because of hard work, knowing the right people and having the magnetism and talent of which stars are made.

But it wouldn't happen overnight, or be easily, or just because some important people were pushing for her.

Determination is a great part of the equation to success in any line of business, any career. Blind determination mixed with everything else one can gather to their treasure chest. Hard work being only a part of it all.

Events had to come together just right!

Joe Schenck did everything possible to promote Marilyn, and even with Ben Lyon's help it was impossible to convince Zanuck that she was anything more than starlet material. He was blind to her talents. He didn't think she would ever be able to act, and possibly he was merely sold on her most famous act of innocence-sexiness. Any woman that "dumb" had to be dumb—this could hardly be an act. Apparently, for him, at lease, she was just too convincing in her role, in her image, in her sell.

He wasn't buying!

But Marilyn continued to pose for as many publicity pictures as she could. At the same time she worked hard studying acting, diction, dancing, doing everything possible to improve herself so that she would, in time, be able to impress the studio "King" that she was something more than just a pretty body to look at. Whenever asked, she appeared in public on publicity assignments. She was in every way the most cooperative starlet who could be found in Hollywood.

Finally she managed to be promoted into a very small film appearance, but the scene ended up on the cutting room floor. Not an uncommon fact of life in the film industry, even for big named stars. Every actor has a story to tell about their best scene ending up lost forever in some film editor's garbage can.

For a starlet, it could be the death of a career.

When everything failed to catch the attention of Darryl Zanuck, and her contract ran out, the studio dropped her.

Such frustration has made many potential stars give up, throw in the towel, feeling there's no chance of getting another break. And for eight months Marilyn was, for all practical purposes, out of the Hollywood scene.

One wonders the pain and torment she might have gone through during this period. Many men and women tossed out like that just give up. A few continue batting their heads against the studio walls only to be brutally battered to failure.

It takes not only determination, but also amazing guts to fight back against all these horrid odds. The walls have been slammed down around the studios. There is no access. Doors are locked shut. You can't even get past the guard standing at the entrance gate. You're dead meat!

One moment success seemed so close, and now it was crushed out of existence. And if you couldn't see the people you were lost.

But Marilyn Monroe was not about to stand there begging, lost, never to be discovered, never to be found by some important person who would open one of those rigidly closed doors. She would do whatever was necessary to beat them at their own game.

She simply would not give up!

She lived on what little savings she had and continued to work as a model, until suddenly that second big break arrived. She attracted Columbia Pictures' attention and was again signed to a stock contract. Once more she found a person willing to promote her career.

This time it was Natasha Lytess, the studio drama coach. The pay-off was a very bad "B" musical called *Ladies of the Chorus,* in which she was assigned two songs to sing.

And now another important person came into Marilyn's life. Freddie Karger, head of the music department, coached her in the two singing numbers for the picture. They quickly became good friends. Marilyn fell hard for this young, attractive man. He not only was good looking and likable, but had that one ingredient important to her: old enough to make him a good father figure. Up to now she hadn't been exposed to the fine arts, and under Freddie's influence she became aware of the world of literature, music and art.

Marilyn not only attracted the attention of the minor VIP's at Columbia, but also of Harry Cohn, who was president of the studio. And he was one of the top casting couch power brokers.

Mr. Cohn had quite a reputation and was not very well liked by many people in town. He used his power to get whatever he wanted. And he was supposed to have been rather crudely brutal in his abuse of other people.

He expected pretty young ladies under contract to please him in any way he might demand. He called Marilyn into his office one day and quite bluntly invited her to a private party on his yacht, just for the two of them.

But she wasn't ready to play this kind of scene—which later would be acted out, tongue-in-cheek, in *Some Like It Hot* with Tony Curtis.

Angered, Cohn threatened that this would be her last chance and that she be smart to reconsider.

But she remained staunch and not long after that the Studio dropped Marilyn. How much her refusal influenced her dismissal is hard to say.

Once again she was out of work, a struggling model with little immediate hope of getting another chance. She had fluffed two opportunities, and it would seem there was even less hope of getting a third chance.

Yet even this disappointment didn't stop her. Determination was, apparently, her middle name. At least, Norma Jean was not about to let Marilyn Monroe die on the vine, so to speak. Normal Jean was determined to make Marilyn Monroe the success she had dreamed about all her life. She would make Hollywood salute her, and make Marilyn famous.

It was during this time that Marilyn posed for the famous calendar picture that would make such a sensation some years later. Though many rumors were circulated about the photograph, it was reported that not only was everything on the up-and-up, but that Tom Kelley, the photographer, had his wife present at the shooting.

Marilyn was paid $50 for this picture, and the money was used to keep her going during this low ebb in her career. She soon forgot it, since it was merely one of many modeling assignments she had accepted—though the first time in the nude.

During this time she was asked to appear in the Marx Brothers picture *Love Crazy,* a part which made no dramatic impression on Hollywood or the world.

Then she met a man by the name of Johnny Hyde. He was twice her age, by far not the most attractive male in her life, in his fifties and suffering from an ailment which would soon take his life. He'd had a heart attack a little before meeting Marilyn. He was known to be one of the nice guys around town. More important, he was a top agent working for the *William Morris Agency* in Hollywood, and his immediate interest in Marilyn turned into love. He had helped a lot of stars make their mark on Hollywood, and had never been involved in any scandal of any kind with them. His love for Marilyn was responsible for the big push he made to promote her career. This was the first man in her life who was really important to Marilyn. Even though Marilyn didn't actually love the man enough to marry him, there was no secret about the fact that they were having an affair, which lasted until his death.

He was a substitute father that she had never had—and also a lover. A difficult role for a man, especially with such an attractive woman. Hyde knew that he was going to die soon and wanted Marilyn to have his fortune. It is to her credit that she didn't give in to this temptation.

It was Johnny's contacts that got her a role in the motion picture *The Asphalt Jungle.* It was a walk-on, but the kind of walk-on designed to project Marilyn's full impact. Her success in this one scene was so great that Johnny was sure that M-G-M, which had produced the picture, would sign her to a contract. It was a great disappointment, both to him and Marilyn, when M-G-M refused, on the grounds that one blonde bombshell was enough for any one studio. Their big blonde star at the time was Lana Turner.

But Marilyn's success and impact in *The Asphalt Jungle* made it possible for Johnny to sell her to Joseph Mankiewicz, who was in charge of assembling a picture for Fox Studios titled *All About Eve.*

Again the part was a walk-on, this time with George Sanders—but *what* a walk-on! The Monroe body and walk were explosive enough to land a second time around with 20th Century Fox. What might have happened after that, nobody can guess. Marilyn had made explosive appearances in two pictures, attracting attention in Hollywood and around the country with merely walk-on roles. The impact of these two appearances was strong enough to create great press. And PR is the name of the game. But at this time Johnny Hyde died, and Marilyn was again left alone in the world of Hollywood. And Fox Studios was still run by a man who just didn't see Marilyn as star material—Zanuck.

It is amazing how short sighted such an otherwise profoundly smart filmmaker could be. What he had against Marilyn is difficult to know; but obviously he was blinded to her impact—one which would soon become evident and make her a major international sex symbol.

Fox Studios had her, but wasn't making any use of her talents.

Thus she was once again floundering, her career in seeming limbo without any strong hand to open doors and influence important people.

Again, Marilyn didn't give up. Norma Jean wouldn't let her. She did the only thing possible for her to do: posed for publicity pictures. And, even if the studio boss wasn't interested, the Fox photographers were more than pleased to have her before their cameras. They knew what their studio boss refused to admit: Marilyn had not only ability and talent, but also a special and powerful impact that could be captured on film. The proof of the power of a good photograph is the popularity, which Marilyn earned during this time. Her pictures were appearing in all of the movie fan magazines. And slowly, at first in trickles, then in full bags, mail started flooding the studio, brazenly acclaiming Marilyn's popularity—a popularity gained by a couple of walk-on roles and hundreds of still pictures being distributed all over the nation. Much to the embarrassment of all her detractors, especially Zanuck and many of the studio's top stars, Marilyn's fan mail was the heaviest on the lot. No matter who was "blind" to the fact that Marilyn Monroe could become a success in motion pictures, the facts were beginning to become obvious even to Zanuck.

It all came to a head one day in a way that couldn't be ignored. There was a large meeting at the studio of all the major film exhibitors from all over the country. Now, film exhibitors, like stockholders, exert a powerful influence on any producer or studio. When the exhibitor's scream for a certain star, Hollywood brass listened. The exhibitors were painfully aware of something that Zanuck still refused to acknowledge. Marilyn Monroe was not only star material, but was already in great demand.

The studio might want to ignore her, and they could refuse to put her in pictures, but the public's interest demanded more of this now very popular sex symbol. They couldn't get enough of MM!

And the Hollywood power brokers couldn't continue to keep their eyes closed to this demand.

Marilyn was fully aware of the popularity the still pictures had created for her. So her appearance at the large exhibitors' meeting had to make a big splash that nobody could ignore. She went to the studio wardrobe and picked out the most attractive, revealing dress she could find.

She was, as far as Fox Studios were concerned, just another starlet designed as background material for the big name stars. Decoration, glittering eye-candy to enjoy, but not to be taken seriously. But Marilyn took this chance very seriously and her impact was stunning. She immediately attracted attention because of her dress and body. And attitude. The Monroe image was being offered in a package that presented it at full blast! And Norma Jean was smart enough to know exactly how to make the most of her Marilyn Monroe!

Everybody wanted to know which pictures she would appear in. They all clamored around Marilyn, asking the same question. Marilyn's short, sharp retort was simplicity in itself.

Louella Parson's quoted the statement thus: *"You'll have to ask Mr. Zanuck about that."*

Imagine his frustration and surprise!

The pressure was on hot and heavy—the kind nobody could ignore, not even the powerful Zanuck. No matter how blind and negative he was to Marilyn's acting ability he was being forced, by immediate events, to deal, in public, with the sudden Super Star Popularity of an unknown, minor, contract player whom he had no plans in putting into any films. And he reacted, as any smart businessman would have.

Blind, but not a fool. It may really have merely been a matter of his attention being distracted by the many products that Fox Studios was involved with during this period. Certainly a contract player, who had next to no screen credits, was of little importance in his world. To him, up to this point, perhaps, she was simply non-existent. After all, he could hardly be expected to take notice of everybody who had a contract with them. He had more important matters to attend to. Like, for instance, the film exhibitors demands.

Zanuck hadn't become such a power broker, such a successful filmmaker by ignoring public tastes. And now he was face to face with the fact that a minor contract player was suddenly a very valuable piece of studio property.

This got his attention!

From that moment on, Marilyn was on her way. With every renewal of her contract the price tag for her services went higher. But strangely enough it wasn't Zanuck or Fox who was responsible for giving Marilyn her first major chance to prove beyond all doubt her ability to not only be popular, but to become a star. It was left to RKO, and Louella Parson's daughter, Harriet, who was making the motion picture *Clash by Night,* which publicized a trio of stars any starlet would be thrilled to work with: Barbara Stanwyck, Paul Douglas and Robert Ryan. And while Marilyn's part was small, it was important, both to the picture itself and for her career.

Harriet, who was producing the picture, first thought of Marilyn as being much the same off screen as she had been in the still pictures and past films, but soon learned, much to her surprise, that there was depth to the young sexy starlet. During this period Marilyn brought thick philosophy books to the set which she studied while waiting to do her scenes. Some of the frustrations of working in films, which all actors experience, regardless of their importance, are the long periods of waiting to be called before the cameras. They might be given orders to arrive at the studio as early as six in the morning, to be made up, and yet might not be called to perform until late in the afternoon, or many times, not at all.

Throughout her life Marilyn searched for a true, happy place for herself, for love and contentment. She went through periods of reading and studying thought-provoking books. It was a pattern that revealed the hopeless search for something that the world never truly gives to anybody: perfect happiness and contentment.

We can only reach for this limitless goal; yet never totally embrace its rich rewards.

Life at best, for all of us, is a series of struggles for those moments of happiness, those flowers in a parched and thirsty desert. And like many who were much like herself, Marilyn was never to find what she was looking for. Being sensitive and aware of her own faults, unable to compromise with the reality of life, she ultimately found this to be one of her most important and painful failures.

Marilyn especially studied the human mind in her hunger to gain greater understanding of mental illness. Since her mother and mother's parents had gone insane, she was terrified that she might inherit this same illness, even though doctor's always assured her that insanity was not hereditary.

It was during the filming of *Clash by Night* that Marilyn started her tardiness routine. It was a habit that was to plague her for years to come. She also started another practice: demanding that her personal coach be present when she was performing—at this time it was Lytess, who had been a friend of hers since the making of *Ladies of the Chorus.* She was given private direction from Lytess on every scene and followed this advice. How much responsibility can go to Lytess for Marilyn's success in *Clash by Night* will never really be known. Marilyn had a natural talent, which might have projected itself without the personal coaching. Yet she seemed to desire this kind of personalized attention. The fact remains that this was her first real all-out success in a motion picture film. To this point her roles had been either too small to show her full potential or in such bad, low-grade movies as to have gone unnoticed. In *Clash by Night,* Marilyn hit pay dirt, at top gear, unexpectedly outshining the three stars who had been big box office for many years. There was no question now that Marilyn Monroe was going to be as big in movies as she had been in still pictures. Of course, nobody knew that she would be the biggest thing to hit Hollywood in the 1950s, and for that matter, possibly for all time. Even today she's a legend.

Critics and fans alike acclaimed her success. She captured almost all the rave reviews.

Then, unexpectedly, something she had done four years before caught up with her. Suddenly it appeared as if everything she had worked for might backfire and go up in a blaze of scandal and smoke.

The calendar nude of Marilyn had been released some time before, but since she had been an unknown, it had made no more impression than a thousand other such pictures. Now, suddenly, it appeared in a blaze of color, publicity and whispering rumors.

There is a moral clause in every Hollywood contract, which, if necessary, can be put in effect if there is any question about "morality" of the star in question. It is, to all effects and purposes, a mere legal safeguard, but in the case of Marilyn Monroe it could have canceled out not only her contract, but her career as well.

Some years later, when Marilyn was making *Some Like It Hot,* she sent autographed copies of this calendar photo to several friends, on which she wrote: "I hope men like me better with long hair." By then, of course, it had become legend.

Even *Playboy* magazine used the picture in its center spread, and this proved to be one of the most popular Playmate pictures it had ever published.

But in the beginning, when the news got out that this was, in fact, Marilyn Monroe, it was a shattering experience for the young actress.

For her, posing for the picture was something in the past and certainly not considered anything but a means to pay the bills. It was one of endless photo-sessions she had done for countless photographers.

The fact that the public not only enjoyed nude photography, especially of an up-and-coming young starlet, but couldn't care less about the hows or whys of the picture, is testified by

the fact they couldn't get enough of it. Instead of her career being ruined, it was actually turned into a major plus for her career. Marilyn Monroe, instead of being damaged by the calendar
picture, was literally becoming a major item in the public's
mind. And that's how super stars are made. The public, in the
long run, is the Star maker. When she told the press the true
story about the picture, it not only made good headline material,
but won for her even more acclaim.

The scandal smothered, the picture adored, and Marilyn
acclaimed for her role in *Clash by Night,* finally convinced
Zanuck, beyond any doubts he still might have embraced, that
he had a gold-mine in Marilyn Monroe. And gold mines needed
to be tended. After years of struggle, failure after failure, frustration after frustration, but never once really giving up hope,
Marilyn Monroe was back at the studio, which had been the
first to sign her and drop her. She was finally on her way.

Marilyn Monroe, at the beginning of her career almost
suffered another shattering scandal. Jerry Karpman and Morrie
Kaplan, who had never known Marilyn any more than they
knew the man in the moon, and who were in the business of
sending out pornographic pictures of supposedly famous movie
stars, had picked Marilyn as an outstanding subject for their
filthy business.

They would contact possible clients to promote their
pornographic picture business through the mail. In Marilyn's
case, they sent the following letter:

> Hello there, my name is Marilyn Monroe.
> I hope you don't think me too bold for writing,
> but it is out of necessity that I do. I am out of a
> job and I have to raise some money quickly.
> Therefore, I have had to do something that I
> never would have done under ordinary condi-
> tions. A short time ago two friends of mine and
> myself got together and took some pictures...
> They got a lot more enjoyment out of it than I
> did. But, of course, that is only natural. Marilyn
> Monroe.

It was handwritten, in feminine handwriting, and from all outward appearances seemed authentic.

The Los Angeles police became aware of their activities and arrested Karpman and Kaplan, then sent a subpoena to Fox Studios in the name of Mrs. Norma Jean Daugherty, so as to save Marilyn any unpleasant publicity. She was one of the D.A.'s star witnesses. Appearing in court in a robin's egg blue skirt and jacket and open-toe shoes, Marilyn was questioned on the witness stand.

"Is this handwriting yours?"

"No," Marilyn firmly announced.

"Did you write this letter?"

"No."

"Did you authorize anyone else to write it?"

"No."

Her evidence at the trial was responsible for sending Jerry Karpman and Morrie Kaplan to jail for long sentences.

This was not the end of the story but merely the prologue. The worst was yet to come.

Some time later, when a carload of pornography was picked up by the authorities, several policemen were going through it, and one of them found an envelope in which were quite a few pictures of what appeared to be Marilyn Monroe in highly intimate poses with a man. The policeman saw a chance to cash in on what he considered good fortune for himself.

Crooked "cops" are, regardless of some bad publicity, exceptions. Policemen and women are badly underpaid and have to deal with dangerous situations on a daily bases. Nobody, one might claim, put a gun at their heads forcing them to become officers of the law. And, for the most part, they don't complain and do their jobs in a dedicated and caring way. It's a tough business. And except for a few bad examples, these are dedicated, underpaid, men and woman who many times give up their lives to protect the public.

But there are always, in all branches of society, those who abuse their power for illegally profits. It's an unpleasant fact that even within government, within the very structure of the police force, there are those who deal in graft, who accept under-the-table payments, pay-offs. There is no secret about this. Crooked politicians who literally own the heads of the police department, and thereby control the law have run entire towns. But these are exceptions.

One day Marilyn answered the door to find a policeman standing there. He showed her the pictures, and suggested that it could go hard on her if they were made public. He suggested that he'd be willing to see to it that they were destroyed if Marilyn would offer some reward.

Marilyn, terrified, didn't know what to do, but managed to put the man off, to give herself time think it over.

The office kept calling Marilyn, to remind her of the ax he held over her head.

Marilyn was afraid to pay the man off and at the same time terrified to go to either her studio or the police. But finally she realized that the only thing she *could* do was asked her studio for advice.

Much to her surprise the studio merely asked if she had really posed for the pictures, and when she assured them she hadn't, the D.A.'s office was quickly notified. It was only a matter of a short time until the officer was in custody. The pictures discovered in his desk were so skillfully faked that it was impossible to say, for sure, they weren't real. Lab tests were made, but apparently revealed no solid proof. In the end, through an oversight of the people who had originally made the pictures, a birthmark was discovered on the woman—a mark, which Marilyn herself didn't have. This fact closed the issue forever, leaving Marilyn with merely the memory of one of many unpleasant experiences.

All this took place in August 1952, and could have been very harmful to her career, especially considering the publicity which she had been getting from the nude calendar shot that had become such a popular collector's item.

Another little story which involved Marilyn was the rumor that she had a half-sister by the name of Louise Angel, a woman who looked enough like Marilyn to truly be her half-sister. The fact that Angel was a stripper was an embarrassing fact that proved very annoying to Marilyn. The rumor started slowly and then spread so far as to make it necessary for Marilyn to make a statement to the papers to the effect that she did in truth have a half-sister, but that it wasn't Louise Angel. When the stripper was questioned privately about the rumor she proved to be quite ready and willing to back up Marilyn's story. She told the reporter that it had been started by one of her backers as a publicity stunt, and that she had not known anything about it until it was too late to stop the rumor. She was sick of hearing about it, and resented the fact that it had been circulating. She felt her career could do very well without such publicity, since she had been on her own for a long time, and was successful enough not only to regret a connection with Marilyn, but also to be embarrassed about it.

From the moment of *Clash by Night,* and the following success of such movies as *How to Marry a Millionaire,* Marilyn became the national sex symbol until her death.

Also from this time on, Marilyn showed signs of extreme nervousness, which became so acute as to take on physical properties, making her actually sick to her stomach. She would sit talking and her hands would work nervously, the fingers weaving in and out. Her lateness on sets might easily be explained by this nervousness which grew stronger and stronger as time went on. She had a driving desire for perfection, yet the fear of failure. The nervousness that plagued her caused Marilyn to fluff lines in simple scenes again and again. Her insistence on having her personal drama coach on the set with her at all times is an indication of insecurity, as if she were leaning on someone else, and couldn't stand on her own two feet.

It was in 1952 that Marilyn met Joe DiMaggio, one of the most famous baseball figures of all time. Joe was a basically simple man who had simple desires. He would date Marilyn and take her out on long rides, or they would sit together and watch television in the evening, alone, away from the world, which adored both of them. Joe wasn't the kind of man who delighted in constant publicity. His love for baseball, no doubt, had driven him into his profession, but his own personal desires for privacy, home and family, were his basic motivations in life. In this way Joe was different from any other man Marilyn had known. But in another, more important way, he had a basic appeal, which was one of the first requirements for a Marilyn Monroe husband: old enough to serve as a father image.

One thing that puzzled Hollywood, and the baseball world alike, was the fact that to all outward appearances they had little or nothing at all in common. Marilyn Monroe, public domain, sex symbol of the movie world, and Joe DiMaggio, hero of the baseball diamond. Yet, strangely, in the end, it was Joe who turned out to be the only real long-lasting man in her life, a man whom she went to years later, after her divorce from Arthur Miller. There was something about him which responded to Marilyn and to which she responded. And this couldn't, even after many years, be forgotten. It was a link, which bound them all their lives—and even after her death Joe was dedicated to Marilyn's memory.

It was during the time that Marilyn was dating Joe that she won the *Photoplay* award for the "Best New Star". This top fan magazine, when it gave out its annual movie awards, had a festive dinner to celebrate the occasion. Marilyn, true to form, arrived two hours late. Her tight-fitting, gold lame dress won the approval of all fans present, regardless of the fact that the Hollywood set was shocked and amazed by the revealing gown that clung to her as if it had been painted on. It was so tight that Marilyn had difficulty even walking, and, much to the delight of her fans, it was all too obvious that she had nothing on underneath her dress.

Joan Crawford, a lady famed for her taste in dress, was most critical of not only the young starlet's dress, but the whole performance. Her opinion was highly respected in Hollywood, but especially so by Marilyn who had very much admired the actress because she appeared to be such a devoted and outstanding mother.

Joan was quoted by Louella Parsons as bluntly saying:

> It was like a burlesque show. The audience yelled and shouted, but most of us in the industry just shuddered...Miss Monroe should be told that the public likes provocative feminine personalities, but it also likes to know that, underneath it all, the actresses are ladies...

The fact that Marilyn was so deeply hurt by this, not only reveals her honest respect for Joan Crawford, but also her intense desire to be loved by everybody. [Sadly, for her, at the time little was known about the real Crawford style of parenting, which, apparently, was far from that of a doting mother.]

During this time, while still dating Joe, Marilyn was sent to Niagara Falls, to make the motion picture *Niagara* in which she played a hip swinging sex-pot, hardly her best part. But effective. One night, it was reported, a reporter by the name of Bob Slatzer turned up at her rooms in the General Brock Hotel, where she was staying in Ontario, to interview her.

If she was drunk, lonely, having an unexpected fling, or merely practicing a long standing habit of having casual affairs can never really be known.

But from all reports, Mr. Slatzer got more than a merely a personal interview.

The timing of this relationship with Bob was interesting. Did it suggest that Marilyn was simply "running wild"? Does it imply that she had been playing the casting couch game all along? Or, perhaps, was simply a woman enjoying casual affairs? Or desperately seeking love in the arms of any man who attracted her?

It is quite impossible to know. Mr. Slatzer, some years later, published a book that fully developed these events, along with the claim that Marilyn was murdered. According to him an affair turned into a short-lived marriage.

The fact that she became intimate with this reporter might suggest a casual approach to sex.

Or was she simply seeking the man who might spark a real fire in her? In other words: had her early sexual experiences as a child, being raped, told that sex is "dirty" made her really rather frigid?

Perhaps she was attempting to live up to her public image as a sex idol! A lame-brained dumb blonde who slept with any man who turned her on?

Or was this image of a hot sexy lady a real reflection of Norma Jean?

Of course, nobody can really know; not even her most intimate male partners. Men have been fooled by women who skillfully "fake it"! And Marilyn was, after all, a skilled actress. Only she could answer truthfully about her sex-drive—and about what was true and false concerning her real relationships. The public believes what it wants to.

The real Marilyn Monroe, Norma Jean, lived with her own inner demons.

But, of course, Bob was not the first, nor was he to be the last of her reported bedroom adventures with men. Nick Ray, a Hollywood director, was another reported lover of Marilyn. It is true that some people enjoy a series of love affairs with many different partners, but surely there is a big difference between love affairs and mere affairs.

With Bob Slatzer was she just out for a kick? A last minute thrill before she married Joe? No one can know for sure, but one fact becomes strongly clear to anyone taking the time to study the complete pattern of her life: *Marilyn, in and out of marriage, was suspected of sharing more than one man's bed during any period of time.*

But her relationship, however intimate or involved, with Mr. Slatzer, was short-lived. Marriage or not! It came to a quick enough end, leaving her free to pick up the far more lasting relationship with very famous person: Joe DiMaggio.

Marilyn's relationship with Joe didn't change until after she ran out on the production of *The Girl in Pink Tights*. She had become disgusted with her situation at the studio, which by now had become deadlocked. She had no control over the scripts and was not receiving proper financial rewards for her efforts, which her fame surely should have demanded. Frank Sinatra, who had been hired as her co-star was to be paid far more than Marilyn, a fact which finally was partly responsible for this walk-out.

Norma Jean had fought hard in her climb up the ladder of success, never giving up, no matter how difficult things became. And nothing was going to stop the bomb-shell Marilyn Monroe!

This was to be her first of many all-out battles with the studios over money and recognition.

The studio retaliated by suspending Marilyn—a situation that didn't seem to bother her in the least. If she didn't work, they said, they wouldn't pay out any money. Marilyn seemed to feel she had enough money to be independent for such a period of time as was necessary to get her way.

And she had another shock to offer the world!

Louella Parsons was given the honor of breaking to the world the news that Marilyn Monroe and Joe DiMaggio would become man and wife.

The lovers had ended up in San Francisco, appeared before a Justice of the Peace for a quiet, unpublicized marriage. From there they went to Japan for a honeymoon. While there, Marilyn, always aware of what had made her popular and how to indirectly let her studio know how little she needed them, appeared before the service men in Japan.

It was one of those days when nobody in their right mind would appear outdoors without warm covering. But, Marilyn, knowing what the boys in the service really wanted to see, her body, and as much of it as the law would allow, did her best to keep from disappointing them. Her reward was a persistent cold, which followed her to the States, on her return from Japan.

Joe and Marilyn made no secret about the fact that they wanted very much to have children. But it was part of the tragedy of the Monroe story that she was never to have a child.

In the beginning, Marilyn did everything she could, within reason, to make the marriage a success. She attempted to fit herself into Joe's life, while, at the same time, not wanting to ruin her own career. There was a conflict of interest even in the beginning. Joe would go out of his way to avoid socializing with the Hollywood set. He still wanted those long quiet drives alone with his wife and simple evenings watching television. He didn't want to become involved with the glamorous career of Marilyn Monroe. He wanted a wife by the name of Mrs. DiMaggio, nothing more, nothing less. It was Norma Jean he wanted. But he was married to the public legend.

There were many times when Marilyn had to appear in public, and in the way the public most wanted to see her, alone and revealingly dressed. They still wanted to believe Marilyn, the innocent seeming blonde sex-pot, could be theirs to enjoy, and on their terms: a sexual fantasy. On these terms a married Marilyn was, at best, a problem.

And this MM image was her business, her career, and regardless of anything else she might have desired, her life.

Norma Jean had invented a creature nobody could live up to. One that would, in the end, become the seeds to her own destruction.

She had been reinstated by her studio, but, according to some authorities at a price of $450,000, paid under the table. While Joe resented being out with her in public, he also disliked it when she was appearing alone. This was one of the basic difficulties that would, in the end, be the major force that would end their marriage. At one time he refused to escort her to a premiere, mainly because of the dress she was to wear: a hip and breast clinging gown which she was actually sewn into.

This inner conflict of Joe's is understandable to any man. Obviously he was proud of his beautiful wife, and pleased that she was so attractive to men. Such a situation would be a big ego blast to any man. But there are limits to how much a person can take. It is one thing for a man's wife to appear attractively dressed in public, but quite another when she is wearing a gown that is designed for the specific purpose of creating raw, burning desire in each man who sees her. She was dressed to kill. Dressed to seduce every man into wanting to take her to bed. That was her business. This was her image. The hot, sexy lady who was easily seduced into casual sex with any man who might want her.

An illusion. A lie. But a public image which was a big money maker.

And a possible disaster for a successful marital relationship.

Perhaps there were other reasons for Joe's doubts and frustrations.

Both of them were famous people, with their own fans and the public adored them. But where Joe's fame was basically limited to a very large baseball audience, Marilyn's was international fame on a very broad scope! Not merely within a sports arena. She was plastered around the world in revealing photos, her body on easy display, and the studio publicity department was out to make the most of her image as the most desired sexy woman in the world.

Marilyn Monroe was in demand, worldwide. Every man, supposedly, had sexual fantasies involving her. And her naked body was in full display, in the nude calendar photo and Playboy centerfold. Beyond that, Marilyn was a woman and the female of the species will always attract more attention than the male—at least publicly in the press.

With all honesty, it must have been difficult for both of them. Joe's reluctance to go around with Marilyn during her business appearances, is reported by Hedda Hopper, wherein she experienced having Marilyn come to her home for an interview, and Joe staying outside in the car, waiting. He had told Marilyn that he would knock on the door when it was time to go.

There was every reason to believe that Marilyn didn't stop her extra-marital affairs even when married to Joe. This is accentuated by the fact that Joe and Frank Sinatra (a close friend of the baseball player) had Marilyn followed one evening by private detectives. When she went into an apartment, Frank and Joe were notified and hurried there at top speed, went to the door, which the detective pointed out, and broke into the apartment. Much to their surprise and embarrassment, it turned out to be the wrong apartment, but Marilyn heard about it and blew her top.

More evidence that Marilyn was sleeping out on Joe is the belief that it was Marilyn's affair with her vocal coach, Hal Schaefer, which caused their divorce.

Though such stories have been so-called "common fact," it must be pointed out that nobody other than the people involved could actually know for certain what really went on in the intimate privacy of their homes. But, on the other hand, it is difficult to believe that such stories were nothing but the fictional gossip of people with dirty minds.

Marilyn Monroe had always attracted male attention. Her life as a professional actress was devoted to being a high-powered man-trap, and her constant involvement with lovers, between her marriages, would seem to testify to the truth of all these fairly reports of her relationships other men.

There is no doubt that the conflict between Marilyn's career and the demands it made on her life, and the desires of her husband to have a wife who wasn't in the public domain, was complicated by Joe's own understandable suspicions. He had good reason to believe the stories of her secret meetings with other lovers. And this was enough to shake the foundations of any marriage.

If the relationship between Marilyn and Hal Schaefer was in fact a swinging affair, it could have been that this was the last straw.

But there were also other little straws that helped to weaken the marital relationship. It was during the production of *The Seven-Year Itch* (in which, according to Hedda Hopper, Marilyn perfected the delivery of double meaning lines) that some of the marital conflict came to a head.

The famous skirt-blowing scene of the movie was shot at Lexington Avenue, the East 50s, a fashionable section of town. It was August 1954 at 2:30 in the morning. The cameras were set, the crew ready, and the director was talking to Marilyn. Joe DiMaggio was lost to one side, amid a crowd of some 4,000 fans who had gotten word of this secret shooting location. Marilyn was standing over the subway grating on the sidewalk under which had been placed a large fan that could be turned on at will—making it unnecessary to await a train that might and might not give the camera the needed effect. When the director gave the word the camera was moved into action. The slate snapped in front of the lens and the fan under the sidewalk grating turned on full force, pushing the skirt away from Marilyn famous, attractive legs.

Men consider this, one of the sexist poses any actress might offer up for a publicity shot. It has become famous!

Joe, as has been pointed out, felt a certain amount of understandable uneasiness about the blatant exposure of his wife's beautiful body to the public that was all too eager to see and worship it.

This time he was present for a first-rate showing of how the movie fans responded to his wife. And what a good showing it was!

Marilyn wore only skin-tight panties under the dress, and the fan was giving everybody around, except Joe, a lot of fun and excitement studying those wonderfully shaped legs. And, perhaps, hoping to see far more than was expected to be exposed.

It must have been a painful experience for a man of Joe's sensitivity to be standing there, off to one side, unnoticed, watching the crowd hypnotized by his wife's body and legs. The mass desire of the crowd must have been humiliating to him.

During all this, Joe revealed his dislike of the proceedings to a reporter who asked how he felt about it. His answer, according to the reporter, was the ever-popular evasion of: "No comment!"

Two months after the shooting of this scene, their marriage was finished. How much, if any, this had to do with the final breakup, is doubtful, but surely it added its black mark.

Joe gave Norma Jean a choice, when she finished making the picture. Either she could be the glamorous public image called Marilyn Monroe, or settle for the less popular role of merely being his wife: Mrs. DiMaggio.

It was the kind of demand which could have only one reply, then or ever, for no matter how much she might have hated the Marilyn Monroe image, at times, it was hers for life. In an almost literal way Norma Jean had become Marilyn Monroe.

In 1955 Marilyn was awarded her divorce on the all-embracing grounds of mental cruelty, and so ended another important phase of her life.

The shattering result of the breakup of her marriage, and the success of the motion picture *Seven-Year Itch* apparently had its effect on Marilyn. It was during this period that she again became very unhappy with her position at the studio, and decided it was time to put some real pressure on 20th Century Fox to gain the recognition now due her.

Some say that it was a sense of insecurity, complicated by the continued advice of so many people around her which, though no doubt given in good faith, not only confused her but finally caused Marilyn to leave the studio and form a personal corporation. Now she hoped to produce her own movies, over which she would have complete control. Milton Greene, a New York photographer, with no experience in the making of motion pictures, was highly responsible for this move. He helped her form the corporation, which was organized to do battle with Fox. The Greenes were good friends of Marilyn, and it is understandable that she would listen to their advice, regardless of the fact that Greene, himself, was fairly close to personal-bankruptcy. Some people felt that Marilyn was out of her mind to turn away from those very people who were responsible for having made her the big-name star she had become. Yet that was what she had done. And while it is true that the Hollywood experts probably knew what they were doing, having had long experience in the making of stars, it can also be understood that Marilyn had every reason to resent them. After all, in the beginning, it was this same studio which had been so blind and so reluctant to even give her any real chance at stardom.

While Marilyn was on suspension from Fox, living in New York City with the Greenes, she appeared on the Ed Murrow *Person to Person* television show. And according to Hedda Hopper she bombed out completely. While others assured Marilyn that she had been and looked wonderful on the show, it was Mrs. Hopper who had the honesty and candor to express her own negative feelings about the appearance.

This, surely, had a tendency to confuse the already insecure Marilyn. She was still top press in the national newspapers and fan magazines. And, if that had been possible, fans would have fairly torn the clothing off her body when she appeared in public. She was forced to play a cloak-and-dagger game in order to merely do simple things that other women throughout the nation take for granted. A pair of dark glasses and a black curl-fringed turban served as a perfect disguise for window-shopping in New York City, or visiting such cafes and theaters as attracted her attention.

Marilyn was going through a period of life where she was again searching for something which even fame and fortune hadn't been able to bring her. Her career, as far as making pictures was concerned, was at a standstill, deadlocked, because 20th Century Fox refused to allow her to make any pictures except for them. She lived, as much as possible, a secluded life, at times with the Greenes in Connecticut, and at other times in a large suite at the Waldorf Towers. Rumors that she was, in fact, being kept by one of several millionaires made good press, but were only rumors.

Trapped by the Fox contract, which had another three years to run, Marilyn had decided the best thing she could do was to merely refuse to do any picture at all.

To make good use of the time, Marilyn started studying serious acting at the Strasberg Actor's Studio in Manhattan where she was exposed to what has been called "the Method". This was a style of acting that had influenced such famous actors as Marion Brando and James Dean.

Lee Strasberg felt that Marilyn's constant state of nervousness was an indication of great and deep sensitivity, which nobody had to that time actually made any effort to bring out. He now did everything he could to help her to understand and use this sensitivity in her acting performances.

Paula Strasberg, Lee's wife, told Louella Parsons that Marilyn tried to achieve a perfection that was almost impossible for anybody. *"She constantly,"* Paula was quoted as saying, *"seeks it even at the expense of her health and peace of mind."* It was Paula who finally replaced Lytess as Marilyn's personal coach.

The profitable effect of the Strasberg "method" was proven when Marilyn made *Bus Stop.* This was her first movie on return to 20th Century Fox. The replacement of Zanuck by Buddy Adler was responsible for the studio finally giving in to Marilyn's demands. *Bus Stop,* directed by Joshua Logan, was a critical success for the actress.

It was during this period of her life that Arthur Miller became important to Marilyn. Some years earlier she had met him at the commissary on one of the lots where she was working. Cameron Mitchell was with her at the time, and he had been in Miller's play, *Death of a Salesman,* and was responsible for introducing her to Miller.

This event happened a little before her marriage to Joe DiMaggio.

Now, while living in the East, Miller started going out with Marilyn. She married the author in 1956, Miller ending a fifteen-year marriage to become Marilyn's husband.

In the beginning Marilyn claimed to be attracted to Miller because she thought of him as brilliant, and no doubt she was fascinated by the fact that this type of man would find her desirable and lovable enough to want her as his wife.

It was, again, a strange mating.

She was on a self-improvement kick, and this marriage certainly fitted in with this new idea of herself and what she was searching for in life. And Miller, like all her other husbands, had the important requirement of being some years older than herself.

What must, at first, have intrigued her, turned out to be one of the major forces that would finally break up their marriage some years later.

Miller was anxious to help in broadening her culturally horizons. Unlike Joe, he not only felt it right that she continue her career, but actually encouraged her to do so.

The contrasts are striking.

Where Joe was, in effect, too strong in his personal demands on their marriage relationship, determined to live a quiet, private life, away from the public as much as possible, Miller was anxious to help Marilyn reach higher glories as an actress and as a person. Where Joe resented sharing her with the public, Miller went so far as to subdue his own writing career in favor of her acting career.

Miller actually bent over backwards in his attempts to help Marilyn. No doubt, being a sensitive artist, he apparently felt that acting was important to Marilyn and felt that this was her true place in the world, the place that would give her the most happiness.

Her new husband surely influenced Marilyn in many ways. His advice on how she should appear in public had its effect—though it was Marilyn who usually had the last say in such things involving her public image and dress. He believed in her ability and talent as an actress, and encouraged her to continue improving herself. It was, for Marilyn, a complete turnabout. And though, in many ways, her career was moving much more slowly, she was also more selective in choosing pictures.

Miller was a strong-minded, intellectual man, but as it turned out, emotionally not strong enough to give to Marilyn what she truly needed to keep her in complete control. At the same time Miller pushed too hard in his attempts to please Marilyn. Some have felt that Marilyn was really ready to settle down when she married the author. But she was, through his continued encouragement, convinced that this wouldn't give her the full life that could be hers for the taking. Still she tried to become a good housewife, learning to cook, and being an excellent stepmother to Miller's children when they came to visit. She even went so far as to draw a veil over her private life, refusing to allow any photographers near her home.

A friend of Marilyn's said that when Marilyn married Miller, she was "...*ready to settle down. She wanted to have children. She wanted to become a part of his intellectual world. She may even have given some thought to starring in one of his plays.*" And surely, she did in many ways stop being the full-time glamorous star of Hollywood fame. Even her fan mail suffered during this period.

In the beginning of this marriage Marilyn was apparently quite happy simply being Mrs. Miller, and enjoying her adopted children and adopted religion. Miller, not being strongly religious, hadn't thought it necessary that she join the Jewish faith, but Marilyn was determined to go all out, much to the delight of Miller's parents, who were very religious. Considering her background, a childhood where she had never truly belonged to any of the families with whom she lived, Marilyn must have considered it very important to become a part of every phase of Miller's life. During the Jewish holidays it was Marilyn who insisted on burning the traditional Chanukah candles. She even went so far as to learn three new Jewish words every day. Miller would laughingly admit that she was a better Jew than himself.

Other changes were in more simple directions, like taking up gardening, painting in watercolors, writing poems, which she would only show to her husband.

As Mrs. Miller, Marilyn was everything that she believed a wife should be. But when she returned to public life, she did so as the old Marilyn. This woman was in the public domain, living in style. She stayed in a $75 a day hotel suite while in Hollywood. This was the complete opposite of the country house in which the "Miller's" lived. In Marilyn's own words, she described the Connecticut home in this way:

It was

...a very old house, and the former owners aren't sure whether it was built in 1776 or 1783, but they're both important dates when you stop to think about it. The house is kind of an old saltbox with a kitchen extension. We've knocked down several walls, and we're restoring the fireplace with stone from the local quarry in Roxbury. The interior is entirely modern, so far as the furnishings go.

But with all these attempts at domestication, the marriage had its built-in seeds of destruction. Miller, who had at times in the past consulted psychoanalysts, and was by profession a sensitive and intelligent award-winning playwright, should have been aware of Marilyn's real emotional needs. The last thing a woman wants is to get her way, no matter how much she might fight to get her own way, or how willful she might be, or how much of a struggle she puts up. She surely wants to be considered, to have the man take her ideas and wishes seriously, even consult her on important decisions, but she always wants, and needs, a man who will take the lead with her, be strong, firm, while tenderly understanding. She was like a child who wanted to know the boundaries, what the limits are past which it is impossible to move, so that it feels secure in the knowledge of what it can and cannot get away with.

Any psychoanalyst will state that a woman, in many ways, is much the same as a child, in respect to her husband. She will willingly give him her power to make important decisions, secure in the fact that it will be the very best ones for both of them. She had never had this as a child; and had no real role model to follow. Much of what she sought may have been more fantasy than reality—more an imagined concept, rather than a soundly based one. She craved emotional security, love, firmness, consideration. But Miller didn't see it this way. As with any sensitive man, he wished to please his wife, to make her happy, but he saw it as being willing to cater to Marilyn's every whim and desire. No woman can stand the kind of man who bows and scrapes, and lets her hammer him into the ground.

A Hollywood correspondent wrote:

> Anyone seeing Marilyn with her former husband, Arthur Miller, during the days when they seemed madly in love with one another, would have seen her looking at him with the attentive, worshipful gaze of a child regarding a beloved parent, but an intellectual one at that.

Soon after marrying Miller, they went to England to make the picture, *The Prince and the Show Girl* with Sir Laurence Olivier.

Olivier, always the English gentleman who believed that his private affairs are not for the public gaze, who had always been a true professional, never let on in public that during the production of this film Marilyn strained even his English restraint. He was firm when he told the press that working with Marilyn had been a pleasure, and that she was truly an accomplished actress, a fine example of American womanhood.

But awkward events during the filming strained even Olivier's iron nerves. Marilyn would appear on the set, flopping her arms again and again like a crazy duck, in a so-called attempt to "relax her nerves and increase her blood flow". She continued by hopping about the set, claiming that this was an exercise which she'd learned at the Actor's Studio and then even going so far as to keep it up before the camera,

Then Marilyn appeared two hours late on the set one day, with Milton Greene, her business partner, Lee Strasberg, now her dialogue coach, and her press agent, Arthur Jacobs. Olivier apparently found it difficult to hold back his temper. He reportedly, after saying a polite "Good morning", went behind some scenery and kicked the wall.

She made a habit of being late, and at one time angered the director (and co-star) by insisting on more close-ups even when others were completely satisfied with what had already been shot. Olivier's irritation was so great that he was reported to have gone into his dressing room in a silent rage, staying there until it was possible to return to the set in a calmer mood.

To top everything, Marilyn managed not only to be late for her appearances, a long-standing habit by now, but many times didn't show up on the set at all. An associate would call in, saying Marilyn was sick with an upset stomach. One time, after being absent two days, she returned, groggy from sleeping pills—so she said. That day, after continuing to blow her lines, she stopped the shooting to order eight glasses of milk. She claimed that this would get her over the "drugged" hangover.

The difficulties of getting Marilyn onto the set became so hard that it was necessary to often merely shoot around her in order to even get the picture done anywhere near the projected budget.

Considering Marilyn's past history of lateness and sickness before and after acting in front of the camera, and her chronic feelings of self-doubt, it is not hard to imagine that she was, in fact, truly sick from nervousness and fear.

When she returned from England she was quoted as saying that she *now* loved Miller as a man, and not just for his mind.

What an interesting "confession"!

But this attitude toward Miller was to change soon enough. In time she began to realize that the man she believed she had married, wasn't the man who was now her husband. Where before he had seemed the strong, glamorous intellectual playwright, he was now literally her slave. The emotional strength, which she so longed for, wasn't a part of her relationship with Miller.

Still, after returning from England, their marriage was a happy one. When they were out in public, she was Marilyn Monroe, glorying in the fame that had become hers, but at home, she was Mrs. Miller.

Olivier wasn't the only director to have difficulties, but merely one of many.

Billy Wilder was quoted as saying, before working with Marilyn, when warned about her: *"Look, I have an old aunt in Vienna who would be here and all made up at 6:30 in the morning, but she'd stink in the part. Marilyn, contrary to what you think, is absolutely tireless. I'll take her lateness and not my old aunt in Vienna."* Later, after experiencing the problem that was Marilyn Monroe, actress, he admitted that he'd rather take his old aunt from Vienna.

Billy Wilder made both *Seven-Year Itch* and *Some Like It Hot,* and has added this complaint about Marilyn.

"She has breasts like granite, and a brain like Swiss cheese...full of holes. She defies gravity. She hasn't the vaguest conception of the time of day. She arrives late and tells you she couldn't find the studio, though she's been working there for years." And Wilder should know. He was at the receiving end of some painful Monroe antics, which cost a lot of money, a situation which no director, or producer can afford for long. At Samuel Goldwyn studios, Marilyn kept twelve men waiting for her to arrive. She was supposed to record "Running Wild" for *Some Like It Hot.* Two engineers, an assistant director and eight jazz musicians waited along with Producer-director Wilder. Everything had been set up at 1:30. By six in the evening, when she hadn't appeared, Wilder was beginning to get really worried and angry. The assistant director said that he'd been calling since seven in the morning, and had honestly believed she would appear. Another member of the waiting committee commented that once Warner Brothers wanted to invite her to a premiere that started at 8:40. They believed it was necessary to have a special invitation printed for Marilyn that claimed that it was scheduled for eight—and still she didn't arrive until half past nine.

Around seven that evening Marilyn arrived, and by this time almost everybody had just about given up. Some of the men were involved in a gin rummy game. Matty Malneck, the arranger-conductor, was having a meal at a near-by restaurant. Malneck was summoned and when he arrived Marilyn was already in the recording booth, with earphones on, ready to go ahead. They had hardly gotten really started before she suddenly said, through the microphone, to Malneck, *"How do you like the jadda, ja dadda?"* Even though assured by the conductor that it was great, Marilyn suddenly announced, *"I don't think I'm in the mood to sing today,"* and with that left the booth.

During the making of *Some Like It Hot,* Paula Strasberg was again there as companion and personal advisor, much to everybody's irritation. It was reported that Paula attempted to run the show in every scene in which Marilyn was involved, insisting on certain camera angles, seeing to it that Marilyn did her lines "just so," regardless of the director's personal feelings. Paula even went so far as to have special dialogue written into the script.

Such interference from an outside force had a very disturbing influence on the whole production.

To make things worse, Marilyn was going through a period of personal difficulty. She became pregnant, only to have a miscarriage. She was in every way highly irritating to those around her, and especially managed to earn the anger and dislike of her two co-stars, Jack Lemmon and Tony Curtis.

Curtis said: "She's a nasty, un-pleasant dame to get along with. She acts like a prima donna kid—in a school play...she plays everybody off against each other." Tony also claimed that Marilyn told Jack Lemmon she wished she'd ended up with him in the picture. She told both of them that Billy Wilder wasn't as good a director as he used to be. Tony also was reported to have said that the famous Marilyn Monroe kiss was a wash-out. Legend says he felt kissing her was like kissing a Hitler At one point of the conflict between Tony and herself, Marilyn hurled a glass of champagne at his face.

Her relations with Lemmon were also unreasonable. One time when she was standing on the set in bra and panties, waiting for the wardrobe mistress and hairdresser to start their work on her, Lemmon passed by, and like any normal male, gave out with a wolf whistle. Instead of accepting it as it was meant, Marilyn went into a rage. Another reported blow-up between the two came when Lemmon was at the studio cafeteria with several other people from the picture, joking and making fun of the dress he was wearing. Marilyn, upon seeing this, believed he was poking fun at her and said: "1 don't think that's very funny to make fun of the star," then left, going to her dressing room.

Both her co-stars again seem to have insulted her when they played a major prank on the whole production. Rehearsals were being done for the scene where a bunch of mobsters are having a party for their chief, and a giant birthday cake is wheeled in, from which a man leaps with a machine gun, shooting down the guest of honor. Tony and Jack arranged unknown to anybody else, a different kind of surprise; one, which wasn't written into the script.

Everything was ready for a take, but there wasn't any film in the camera, and when the cake was wheeled in, instead of a machine-gunner leaping from it, a beautiful, almost naked blonde leaped out of the cake into full view. Everybody but Marilyn burst into laughter. With an expression of disgust and anger, she turned and stomped off the set and into her dressing room, again thinking that the whole thing had been done to make fun of her.

But they weren't the only ones to have problems with Marilyn. After keeping photographers waiting for two hours, she suddenly arrived, dressed in man's slacks and shirt, with no makeup, only to announce that there would be no pictures that day. When she did pose for them she refused to take on that famous expression of half closed eyes and open mouth which had made her famous. She announced that she was trying to change this conception of herself.

When Marilyn discovered that she was pregnant, she began preparing herself, staying away from the set to rest. Her husband, Miller, presented her with a Zorach statue of an obese nude, which she would proudly point out to visitors who saw it, claiming this would be her in a short while. It surely must have been a shattering experience when she had a miscarriage.

To all outward appearances, Marilyn seemed to have adjusted to the miscarriage, stating that she still had faith in God and believed He would give them children, when the right moment arrived. At least, she told reporters, referring to herself and Miller, that they had each other.

Another example of her super-sensitivity and the pride that she had always felt for her figure is illustrated by this story: While doing the bathing scene for this picture, she had to wear an old-fashioned swimsuit. When she came onto the set, it seemed to everybody there that she was overweight. One of the producers suggested that maybe it would be better if they held off shooting the scene for a couple of weeks, while she lost a few pounds.

She retorted, *"I don't have to. It's just this hippy old bathing suit."*

The next day, to prove her point, Marilyn walked onto the set wearing a very skimpy bikini, which not only revealed almost the entire Monroe figure, but proved beyond doubt to all present that Marilyn was in perfect shape. Her marriage, after *Some Like It Hot* and the miscarriage, was beginning to show the first signs of breaking up. But it wasn't until *Let's Make Love* that it became obvious that the marriage didn't have long to go. Though she still seemed to consider Miller's opinion important, and was, seemingly, from all outward signs happily married.

One example of this daughter-like worship of Miller was played out on the *Let's Make Love* set. It was during the shooting of a rather sexy dance scene—in which everybody on the set had more than enjoyed themselves, and for which she had worn sheer black tights—that she sought approval from Miller. The director was satisfied with what had been shot. This was after many takes, some of which she herself had insisted on. She got her needed husbandly strokes.

Meanwhile she started to become deeply interested in another one of her co-stars, Yves Montand.

When Marilyn had learned that Montand, the seventh choice for the role, had been signed up, she was delighted. Others approached before, were Gregory Peck (who chucked the role when Marilyn announced that she didn't want him to bring his wife on the set), Rock Hudson, Jimmy Stewart, Charlton Heston, Cary Grant and Yul Brynner. Marilyn threw a party at the 20th Century Fox Commissary for Montand, and much to the surprise of everyone, arrived on time, explaining that since she, being the hostess it wouldn't be right to be late. Jerry Wald suggested that maybe he should tell her she was hostess on the set every morning and should be there at 8:00 A.M. to greet cast and crew.

Montand knew, from the beginning that his part, though important, was small, and decided that the only way he was going to be able to make any real impact on the screen was to make the most of what he had, particularly the love scenes. To make things worse, Miller had been hired to expand Marilyn's role.

Marilyn's affair with Yves Montand was no particular secret, and certainly had much to do with her breakup with Miller, later. Marilyn was truly taken by this charming French actor, who was as polished and winning off camera as on. No doubt it wasn't hard for her to fall head-over-heels for Montand, especially considering his romantic brand of lovemaking and undercurrent of complete independence.

Marilyn had always searched for something she never really found, as has been indicated. Here was probably the one man who could prove that sex was all that it had been advertised to be.

Montand was a serious type of person, but he had the typical European male's attitude toward sex, a casual acceptance of it as a basic need of life like eating and sleeping. Also, he was in Hollywood, and his wife, the beautiful Simone Signoret, who won the Academy Award for her performance in *Room at the Top,* was in Paris. His honest love and desire for his wife was proven by the fact that when there was an actor's strike in the middle of the filming of *Let's Make Love* he returned to Paris to be with her while waiting for production to resume.

The first public murmurings of a real-life intrigue between Marilyn and Yves started when it was learned that Marilyn went to the airport with him, sat in the car and drank champagne, until he had to board his plane. They denied any intimacy to the general press, and seemed angered and indignant when the rumors continued. Marilyn, during the production of the film not only refused press interviews, but was also repeatedly absent from the set for reasons of flu, paralyzed nerves, and so-called infection. This cost the studio, according to some authorities, well over $200,000. Louella Parsons reports that Yves told her in private that there was nothing between Marilyn and him. But Hopper tells a different story. Mrs. Hopper reported having seen Yves Montand, sometime after the finishing of the film, the night before he left for Paris to join his wife. He was staying at the Beverly Hills Hotel, and when she was invited to his bungalow, Hopper attempted everything she could do, including making a powerful Martini, to weaken both his reserve and tongue. Yves was refusing all calls from Marilyn. Hopper confronted him with the statement: *"You deliberately made love to this girl. You knew she wasn't sophisticated. Was that right?"*

The French actor retorted with: *"Had Marilyn been sophisticated, none of this would have happened."* His admitted excuse for making love to Marilyn was: *"The only thing that could stand out in my performance were my love scenes. So, naturally, I did everything I could to make them good."*

Between the films *Let's Make Love* and *The Misfits,* there were constant rumors that Montand and Marilyn would end up by divorcing their respective spouses and marrying each other. Like many rumors, this was only partly true. Marilyn apparently believed that this would happen for she did, in time, divorce Miller. Montand remained faithful to his wife, Simone Signoret, to whom he had been married for many happy years.

Strangely, Simone took the whole thing in an amazingly casual manner. She has been quoted as stating:

"I'm sorry about this, because we were friends. I liked Marilyn. You say she loves my husband—I don't blame her, I love him too."

At first, though, she did play along with the attempted denial, which was being put up as a smoke-screen for others who had reasons to believe there was an intimate affair.

> Let us say that Marilyn felt Yves charm—who doesn't? But everything that might be natural among us is twisted and deceived right from the start by publicity and talk. This is what spoils everything between men and women, and not simply between those who are married—

She did, finally give some insight into the understanding of Marilyn's possible reaction to the affair when she said:

> The real problem is that when a woman feels the physical attractions of a man who is not her husband, she must also feel that she is in love to justify it. This makes any affair she might have put her marriage into question. It is no longer casual even if passing—

Marilyn was in for a surprise after her divorce from Arthur Miller when Montand not only made it clear that he planned on remaining married to his wife but actually called it quits with Marilyn. He returned to France, without even so much as a letter of explanation.

Marilyn heard that Montand was to stop off in New York City on his way to Japan where he was to make the film *My Geisha* with Shirley MacLain. She felt that this was her one, and possibly last, chance to confront the man personally, demanding some kind of explanation and hoping that somehow she could convince him that they couldn't live without each other. As it turned out, Montand learned about her plans and changed his, taking another plane which flew straight through.

For years Marilyn had been on sleeping pills, and toward the end was completely dependent upon them, unable to stop even if she wanted to. Anybody able to take as many as twenty pills at a time—a dose which would kill a normal person—would die if they stopped cold. She had also become a chronic hospital patient. John Springer, a close friend and her publicity agent, said that Marilyn went to hospitals like other people called a doctor, and believed that in part this was an attempt to get attention, love and care.

She was, apparently, cured to some extent before making *The Misfits*. But once back in Hollywood she returned to her old habits. When she began work in *The Misfits* it was necessary for John Huston, the picture's director, to take strong measures to get her working regularly. He sent her to the hospital to find out what was wrong after she had started a habit of not coming to work. The doctors reported that she was again addicted to sleeping pills. Marilyn had reached the point where she was taking as many as three on four pills at a time with Bloody Marys and other alcoholic drinks. Huston managed to get her off the pills long enough to finish the picture. It was necessary to substitute other kinds of tranquilizers and keep her under close watch. But when the picture was finished she returned to barbiturates.

Clark Gable, her co-star in *The Misfits,* found the strain of working with her almost impossible to bear.

To Marilyn, working with Gable was a high point in her life. He had been very important in her childhood, and it must have been a thrill to find herself playing his screen-lover. She was like a love-stricken girl.

Her teen-age "father" was now close enough to Marilyn to make it possible for her to see him as a human being. Gable's wife was soon to make him a real father. There was no room for any off-screen intimacies with his co-star, and it is doubtful that there ever would have been. Yet he couldn't have been completely blinded to the explosive seductiveness and real live heat which radiated from Marilyn during the filming of their love scenes in the picture.

Arthur Miller realized that the love scenes, as far as Marilyn was concerned, were real. It must have been highly disgusting and painful to know that his wife was so fully and completely involved with Gable.

Marilyn even blurted out, so all could hear: *"I'm mad about him. I don't see how any woman could help falling in love with him!"*

Marilyn had another tragic miscarriage before the production of *The Misfits* and during the filming of the picture suffered collapse described as "acute exhaustion." She was taken to a Hollywood hospital. It was from here that she made so many calls to Montand, which he completely ignored.

Gable, regardless of the fact that Marilyn was fascinated by him, found the American Sex Symbol so irritating that at one point he exploded, saying, *"By God, I'm going in there and really blow my top to that girl—"*

A few months after finishing the picture he died of a heart attack, which some people, apparently including Marilyn, felt she was in part responsible for, because of the tension and irritation she caused Gable during the production.

An interesting double-play was going on while Marilyn found herself both fascinated by Gable and desperately in need of Montand.

It was during the making of *The Misfits* that Miller met his future wife Ingebord Morath, who had been assigned to take pictures for a French magazine, covering the production of the film. Miller and Ingebord seemed to have hit it off very well, and it was at this time that he learned that she had been sent to a Nazi concentration camp, during World War II, because she had a relative who was involved with the plot to kill Hitler. Her reputation as a photographer was well-established all over the world. She'd been the first person to photograph a harem in the Near East. Later, after the end of his marriage to Marilyn, he apparently remembered the enjoyable times he'd had with Ingebord Morath, for they started going out together, developing a relationship which finally led to the altar.

Some believe that the relationship between Marilyn and Montand was directly responsible for the breakup of the Miller-Monroe marriage, and surely there can be no doubt that it was one of the major influences. Added to her failure to have children and Marilyn's own personal confusion and physical condition, it surely resulted in a situation unbearable to both parties concerned.

Marilyn said later: *"When you put so much into a marriage and have it end, you feel something has died and it has. But it didn't die abruptly. 'Died' isn't the right word for me..."*

And certainly their marriage had had its good times, and no one can question the fact that Marilyn had made an honest attempt in the beginning to make succeed. But as was pointed out, one item of irritation was the fact that Miller had become literally a slave to Marilyn. In the end she had reverted to the old habit of seeing other lovers, and, as with Joe DiMaggio, it became the beginning of the end.

Marilyn obtained a Mexican divorce from Miller. Shortly after that she had another collapse, one which was directly connected with her addiction to sleeping pills. Some close friends were frightened that Marilyn was on the point of taking her own life. She was driven to the Payne Whitney Clinic, in February 1961, registered under the name of Mary Miller, in an attempt to keep her admission to the Clinic a secret. The doctors did all they could to get her off barbiturates by prescribing milder tranquilizers and non-narcotic sleeping pills, a treatment that Huston had found to some extent successful. It was impossible to take her off the pills at once because of the strong dose she'd become accustomed to.

When admitted to the hospital she was taken to a floor reserved for moderately disturbed patients, but when she showed signs of becoming worse, it was found necessary to move her to a section where the most disturbed patients were kept.

Oddly enough, of all the men in her life, it was Joe DiMaggio who stood by her at this time. The closeness of their relationship, regardless of the marriage that had taken place after their divorce, is revealed by the fact that doctors refused to let anyone else see her. They discovered that Joe had a soothing effect on her.

At this point in Marilyn's career, and personal life, she had managed to undergo a series of tragic experiences that were certainly good cause for anybody to feel depressed and lost. Her inability to have children, her guilt feelings concerning possible responsibility for Clark Gable's death, her failure as a woman to find happiness with a man must, by this time, have been completely frustrating. All the fears and doubts which had plagued her since childhood had never been washed away, and were still there to torment her every moment.

She was a heavy drinker and addicted to sleeping pills. Her last movies hadn't been box office successes. Her fear of growing old, fear that her career was slipping away from her all added up to make a woman like Marilyn easy prey to the idea of self-destruction.

While in the hospital, guarded by two private detectives—who some believed had been hired by Joe DiMaggio— Marilyn was reported to have gone into a state of hysterics, breaking a mirror in the attempt to symbolically kill the sex image which had made her so famous. This was the first major hint at what was soon to become a reality, the complete destruction of Marilyn Monroe.

When reporters learned that Marilyn was in the hospital it was thought necessary to have her moved to the Neurological Institute of Columbia-Presbyterian Medical Center, where her treatment was continued until they considered her well enough to be discharged.

After being released from the hospital, Marilyn was a constant companion of Joe DiMaggio, and they traveled to Florida where he was batting coach for the Yankees at their spring training camp. Some four months after leaving the Neurological Institute, Marilyn returned to New York and was admitted to the Polyclinic Hospital to have a gall bladder operation.

Again it was Joe who stood by her side as her only visitor. He rented a plush four-room apartment at Westhampton Beach, on Long Island for her, and there they stayed for some time together. The nation's gossips were predicting Marilyn's second marriage to the baseball player. And just when everybody was convinced that they actually would remarry, Marilyn turned up in Hollywood, alone, and surprised everybody by starting to date Frank Sinatra. For a while some thought that this would continue to the ultimate end, but Louella Parson was right when she said it was nothing but a school-girl crush. Marilyn needed attention, needed to be romanced, and in this field Sinatra was an expert. There was good reason to be surprised by this new match, because it was Frank who had been with Joe, when they'd raided an apartment, expecting to find Marilyn with another man. Actually, Marilyn had made up with Frank during the filming of *The Misfits,* when he was working the Lake Tahoe nightclub.

Not long after this, Marilyn became involved in making the picture *Something's Got To Give.* She was to be paid $100,000 for the film, about one-fifth the amount she was now able to command. She had to do the film at this price because of an old contract obligation. This, in addition to the fact that Dean Martin was making much more, must have been a frustrating. Yet it was a chance to make a real comeback, to prove that her pictures could still make money.

But her personal life had already become too complete of a failure, and her inner insecurity had again become an obsession. She was not only late appearing for shooting but many times actually refused to show up at all.

Her personal fears and doubts must surely have been overwhelming now, for she realized this might be her only chance to make good. Nobody, no matter how popular they might be, could afford a long series of commercial failures. Still, those who witnessed the few days she did appear on the set, felt that she was merely working on one cylinder, that her acting was forced and distant, without depth.

In light of what followed not much later, it became obvious that the end was near, and those around her, who should have seen it coming, not only did nothing to help her, but actually managed to give her the final push she needed to be forced over the edge.

Marilyn worked only five days on *Something's Got To Give,* and wasn't on time once.

According to one Fox spokesman, the studio was faced with some very cold facts. *Cleopatra* had drained the life out of Fox, and they just couldn't afford to have a repeat performance. It was a simple choice of losing their immediate investment (reported to be $2,000,000, but probably closer to $200,000) or take the chance of its running into ten or twelve million dollars. Before the final decision was made, and on the last day Marilyn was at the studio, her thirty-sixth birthday, there was a celebration on the set with caviar and champagne served to both cast and crew. The next day Marilyn didn't appear at the studio. She was reported to be sick. When one day followed another, without Marilyn Monroe showing up, it was too much for the studio bosses. They decided to shelve the picture and fire their leading female star.

Some of the harsh statement made by Fox executives (like Harry Weinstein—who didn't believe she was really sick) surely hit Marilyn hard.

One studio boss said: *"Sure, she's sick. She believes she is and she may even have a fever, but it's a sickness of the mind. It's something she no longer can control. Only a psychiatrist can help her now."*

This announcement added to her own inner fears that she might go insane like her mother. And it must have really climaxed for Marilyn. Two months after her thirty-sixth birthday, on August 5, 1962, Marilyn Monroe was found dead, a victim of an overdose of barbiturates. There will always be some question as to whether she tried to kill herself or not. One newspaper man said, before her death, that Marilyn had had it, and didn't know for sure what might have finished her off; Yves Montand, Miller, Clark Gable's death, or her own inner frustrations. It was noted that the light had been out for a long time, *"and if you ask me, it's never going to go back on again."*

That statement surely pointed the way to what happened to Marilyn in a lonely room, cut off from the world, lost and confused, desperate and defeated by life, by herself, her career, the lovers who had taken her to their hearts only to discover that even their love couldn't help.

And the phone call. Who was it that Marilyn was calling?

In the original publication of this essay, I had written: *Some have suggested, with authority, that there was every reason to believe that she was calling Washington, D.C. Nobody could ever discover the truth, and nobody will ever know.*

But even I knew better at the time and had been warned to not print the truth.

The story of John F. Kennedy's relationship with Marilyn Monroe has been detailed in unlimited articles and books over the decades. Her appearance at Madison Square Garden in 1962, during his forty-fourth birthday bash, where she sang in a breathy sexy voice "Happy Birthday" while wearing tight fitting gown has become a standard film clip used again and again by the media. Many a commentator has suggested that this underscored the fact that they had been involved in an intimate relationship. It has been reported, since their deaths that she appeared at the White House for romantic interludes with the president. She was, supposedly, expecting him to divorce his wife and marry her. If this was truly expressed by Marilyn to anybody it might have merely reflected a very childlike fantasy she embraced. Or did she really have reason to believe he loved her and that marriage was in the offering? This is hard to believe. JFK is known to have had romantic interludes with many women. Right in the White House. These activities were kept private and out of the papers, unlike those of later president's extra-marital affairs. Now it is common knowledge, acceptable historical fact, that John F. Kennedy was somewhat of a playboy right up to the end of his life.

Over the years rumors of all kinds have circulated about his relationship with Marilyn Monroe, including tales that Peter Lawford told about how Robert Kennedy had been involved in the events surrounding Marilyn's death. And even Bobby was supposed to have enjoyed her in bed. In fact, one story tells of how the president literally handed her over to his younger brother in order to get rid of her. Likely story; in fact quite possible. Some men enjoy using their power to seduce lovely woman, and the more powerful they become the greater their desire to enjoy such sexual encounters. Power is a drug and the powerful use it for any possible kind of relationship, including sexual.

The Kennedy males enjoyed their extra-marital affairs. There is no secret in any of it.

There seems to be little question about whom Marilyn was attempting to speak to in Washington. History also suggests she never talked to the president, and that her death may have been a direct or indirect result. Did she know something that could be embarrassing to the president? Could she have been a danger to JFK? Were those rumors based on fact? Was she murdered to keep her silence?

There, again, was endless gossip.

If she died of an overdose of pills, or was in some way "killed" by government agents to keep her quite, will probably never be known for sure. But rumors will continue to exist. Facts will always be illusive. Nor is it of any importance, now.

She had reached, at the age of thirty-six, what seemed an end of her career and the end of the many relationships with the men in her life. What matters is that a woman, famed as Marilyn Monroe, named at birth Norma Jean Baker, had simply, by accident or design, died August 4, 1962.

The mystery of Marilyn Monroe's life and death is certainly one which is plagued with a continuing pattern of a woman seeking something, which she could never find in fame, fortune, love, drugs, or liquor. Her long search for a place of happiness and contentment, for a natural and rewarding fulfillment as a woman and human being had in every way been frustrated. Regardless of her success as one of the biggest Sex Symbols to hit Hollywood in a decade her life had seemed a failure. All this was not enough for Marilyn Monroe, for it lacked that one important element of personal contentment and happiness. A woman possessed with the driving desire for professional perfection, plagued with self-doubts, and never able to come to terms with the world about her. A woman who could not possibly escape the final end, defeat and death.

The very glamour which was a part of the Marilyn Monroe image, the public domain sexpot, not only failed to give her the happiness and security her childhood lacked, but had, in the end, helped to destroy her.

Joe DiMaggio, who took charge of her funeral, refused to allow anyone from the Hollywood crowd to be present during the last rites. She was buried without fanfare, but with a whimper.

A reporter asked a friend of Joe why the man hadn't allowed the very people who had been a part of Marilyn's professional and personal life admitted to the funeral. What the friend said, might in a way, be part of the answer to who killed Marilyn Monroe.

"Would you invite your wife's murderer to her funeral?"

www.ingramcontent.com/pod-product-compliance
Lightning Source LLC
Chambersburg PA
CBHW022017090426
42739CB00006BA/175

* 9 7 8 0 8 9 3 7 0 4 4 4 5 *